Praise for *The Art of Client Service*

"In addition to sage, prescriptive advice, Robert demonstrates the importance of checking oneself with a good, hard look in the mirror—to learn lessons, and strive for greatness in the craft of managing client relationships."

—Sarah Fay, President, Isobar U.S.

"Robert Solomon is the consummate client service guy. His thoughts aren't just applicable to the advertising industry business; I used him to consult with my staff when I was a "client side" person and so much of his thinking is transferable to the consumer public relations arena where I work currently."

—James Allman, Chief Executive Officer,
DeVries Public Relations

"I've spent a career recruiting executives for leadership positions at worldwide companies and advertising agencies. Most either understood the rules set forth in this book or else could have benefited from knowing them. I recommend reading *The Art of Client Service* before your first interview; if you land the job, remember to follow Solomon's advice on your way up."

—Donald C. Gilbert, Founder, Gilbert & Company

"Robert's insights are the difference between good and great. Don't just read it. Memorize it."

—Mark Goldstein, Vice Chairman CMO,
BBDO North America.

"In delicious, bite-sized morsels, Robert Solomon serves up sensible, timeless, advice for distinguishing your brand through generosity of spirit and attention to the most important detail: hospitality."

—Danny Meyer, CEO, Union Square Hospitality Group
and author of *Setting the Table*

"O.K., who else is writing a book?"

ROBERT SOLOMON

THE ART OF CLIENT SERVICE

KAPLAN

PUBLISHING

New York

Vice President and Publisher: Maureen McMahon
Editorial Director: Jennifer Farthing
Acquisitions Editor: Shannon Berning
Development Editor: Joshua Martino
Production Editor: Dominique Polfliet
Production Designer: the dotted i
Cover Designer: Rod Hernandez

Published by Kaplan Publishing, a division of Kaplan, Inc.
1 Liberty Plaza, 24th Floor
New York, NY 10006

Printed in the United States of America

January 2008
10   9   8   7   6   5

ISBN-13: 978-1-4277-9671-4

FOR ROBERTA, AGAIN AND ALWAYS

"He who understands everything about his subject cannot write it. I write as much to discover as to explain."

ARTHUR MILLER

"Writing a book is one of the last chances to do what you want."

TINA BROWN

Foreword by David Verklin xi
Before You Start: And then I got fired . . . xv
Introduction xxiii
    Does Advertising Matter? xxiii
    Why Client Service Matters xxvi

PART ONE The Work

At the start of an assignment . . .

1. Define Success 3
2. Be Multilingual 6
3. Live the Client's Brand 8
4. Agree on a Strategy, a Budget, and a Schedule 11
5. Always Manage Client Expectations from the Outset 16
6. Take the Word *Brief* Seriously 20
7. Know When to Look It Up; Know When to Make It Up 25
8. Make the Creative Team Partners in the Brief 27

9. In Writing the Brief, Provide the Client's Perspective 29
10. Get the Client's Input and Approval on the Brief 32
11. Ask, "What Do My Colleagues Need to Create Great Advertising?" Then Deliver It 35

Looking at creative ...

12. Always Ask, "Does This Advertising Pass the 'So What' Test?" 37
13. Don't Fall in Love with Good Work 38
14. Don't Fall for Bad Work 41
15. Choice Is Good 43
16. Fight *about* the Work with Colleagues, Fight *for* It with Clients 46
17. Do Not Sell 49
18. Bring Your Clients into the Process Early 51
19. Respect What It Takes to Do Great Creative 53

Making presentations ...

20. Client Presentations Are As Important As New Business Presentations 57
21. No Understudies on Presentation Day 60
22. No Scenery Chewers, No Dead Bodies 63
23. Be Prepared to Throw Away the Script 65
24. The More Informal You Want to Be, the More Rehearsed You Need to Be 67
25. Know Your Opening Cold 69
26. Better to Have It and Not Need It, Than Need It and Not Have It 71
27. Support What You Say 73
28. Listening Is More Important Than Talking 75

Running a meeting . . .

29. Start on Time, End on Time 77
30. Have an Agenda and Stick to It (Most of the Time) 79
31. Be Brief, Be Bright, Be Gone 81
32. Lead the Meeting, Don't Tyrannize It 82
33. Always Follow Up 84

PART TWO Relationships

Attitude

34. Judgment Overrides Any Rule 89
35. Credit Is for Creative Directors 91
36. You Cannot Lead an Account from Your Desk 93
37. Avoid the Dark Side 95
38. Great Work Wins Business; a Great Relationship Keeps It 97
39. We Are Smarter Together Than We Are Alone 100

Communication

40. Make No Commitment without Consultation 102
41. There Is No *No* in Your Client Vocabulary 105
42. Before You Tell Clients or Colleagues What You *Think,* Tell Them What You *Know* 107
43. Before You Give Clients What They *Need,* First Give Them What They *Want* 108
44. How to Write a Letter of Proposal 110
45. The Zen of PowerPoint 122
46. In a High-Tech World, Be Low-Tech 129

Trouble

47. Always Think Endgame 132
48. No Surprises about Money or Time 134
49. Deal with Trouble Head-On 137
50. If Things Go Wrong, Take the Blame 139
51. What Happens When I Screw Up? 141

Socializing

52. Remember the Personal Side of Business Relationships 145
53. Take On the Coloration of Your Clients, But Do Not Compromise Your Character 150
54. No Matter How Social It Becomes, Never Forget That It's Business 152
55. Once a Client, Always a Client 154

PART THREE Style and Substance

56. Make an Investment in Your Personal Style 157
57. Invest Some Time (Again) in These Books 161

One more thing . . .

58. Remember to Say "Thank You" 166

After You're Done: What Makes a Great Account Person? 169
Index 177

"Can you put more nudity in this?"

I wish that I had written this book. I should have. I could have. Many of us could have. But only Robert Solomon did it.

I am sure Robert has heard these words many times since he introduced *The Art of Client Service* in 2003 and its predecessor, *Brain Surgery for Suits*, in 2000. Each and every one of us in the advertising and marketing services business should be using the concepts in this book. The ideas discussed within these pages are simply universal and timeless. Whether you are a junior account person just starting out or the leader of the largest independent media planning and buying operation in the world, *The Art of Client Service* applies to what we do right now, right here, every day.

Like Robert, I come from the business side of advertising. And like hundreds of other industry professionals, for every experience he shares in the book, I have a similar example, both positive and negative. That is why this book is a must-have tool for anyone working with clients. At Carat, we've purchased hundreds of copies of Robert's books and made them required reading for our account managers.

Robert was the first advertising industry professional to record the concepts that will make us better account people, and he is among the few who are willing to share with readers examples of what not to do. Robert encourages young, rising professionals not to repeat the mistakes of the past. And with this book, he shows readers old and new to the industry how to avoid those mistakes.

One of my favorite stories about *The Art of Client Services* is one that I've told many times. One of our senior account managers at Carat approached me after I sent him a copy of Robert's book. He strode up confidently after a meeting and said he'd just finished reading the book on a flight from Los Angeles. It's a pretty short and easy read, he remarked. He added there wasn't one thing in the book that he didn't already know, and he didn't understand the hoopla and praise I had heaped on it.

I looked at him and simply said, "Good. Now go out and do it."

That's the great thing about Robert's writing and the book itself. It's full of practical common sense and information we can apply in our day-to-day roles. Like the famous Nike slogan, the key is to "Just Do It."

The book has had a major impact on me and the organization that I lead, Carat Americas. When I arrived a few years ago, Carat was in the middle of growth spurt. We had surpassed 1,200 employees, expanded to 20 offices around the world, and had annual billings exceeding $5 billion. Despite this growth, I was concerned about one thing: client service. While I was happy with our growth, I was troubled because our growing team, our work, and our success could overshadow the most important thing in our business—our clients.

With that in mind, I invited Robert to present at the Carat Management Conference. I gave Robert the charge to make the case for client service to more than 300 of Carat's senior management team. Certainly, we were all content with Carat's success and felt we had been doing many of the right things to help our business and our clients. The challenge was, "How do we build upon the momentum and keep the success from going to our collective head?"

The book and Robert's presentation reinforced a focus on client service that keeps us headed in the right direction. The people in the room were reminded why client service matters, and they took that message to their teams throughout Carat. Since then, I have been an advocate of *The Art of Client Service,* frequently passing out copies to employees and referencing its concepts in presentations and meetings.

One of the things that Robert often talks about is the first rule of client service: "no surprises." In *The Art of Client Service,* you will find no surprises; rather, you will find unchanging concepts and simple anecdotes that will remind you what you can do to create great work, build strong client relationships, and become a great account person in any service organization.

Regardless of how many versions of the book Robert publishes, the foundation of *The Art of Client Service* is the same: client service matters.

I have only one more thing to say, and it follows the advice in the final chapter of this book: thank you, Robert.

David Verklin
CEO Carat Americas
Chairman Carat Asia-Pacific
May 2007

And then I got fired . . .

"Work with us, we're trying to screw you."

And I found myself out of work for the first time in more than 20 years. But I'm getting ahead of my story. Let me start at the beginning.

After six-plus years at Ammirati Puris Lintas, most recently as president of its direct and interactive divisions, I set out on my own. I had been working for others—

before Ammirati at Foote Cone & Belding and before that at a predecessor to the agency known as Digitas—but I wanted to see if I could put my name on the door of something that was mine.

I founded Solomon Strategic in 1999. At first, business was great; I had lots of clients, including the agency I'd just left. Just as one assignment would end, I would get another client's call. Business was easy; I actually felt halfway smart.

But those were the late '90s, when almost everyone dreamed of the next big idea and the private equity firms were the tooth fairies. It was as if every new venture could find a backer with an open checkbook.

One day, my friend Phil Palazzo called to say, "I've got the money to launch an idea, now all I need is the idea." My response was, "If you have the money, I sure as hell have the idea." With that, Phil and I founded what would be the first design-centric holding company—The Design Communications Group—backed with private equity from Jordan Industries.

Phil and I spent a year building the business. In August 2001, we were about to close on our first two acquisitions when Jordan ran into "capital allocation" problems (whatever those are) and pulled the plug on our venture. We were surprised by the suddenness of the change, but Jay Jordan was generous and accommodating, and we parted on good terms.

But if our idea was going to evolve from a PowerPoint presentation to a business, we would need another backer. With Jordan's support, we trolled for a new venture capital partner.

Then, on a beautiful late summer morning, as I was about to head uptown from my lower Manhattan apartment, my wife Roberta reported a frightening, thunderous sound overhead. "Something awful just happened," she said.

We turned on the TV: a report from the World Trade Center, soon followed by another. We watched from the street as the South Tower fell. It was September 11, 2001.

The vastness of the tragedy was overwhelming and incomprehensible, but the fallout, for us, was real and immediate. For starters, there would be no new financing, no Design Communications Group. There would be no new consulting, either, as advertising sought to regain its footing in the wake of a disaster.

After a few months of futility, Phil and I agreed we had to focus on something more pressing than private equity: finding jobs.

So in the summer of 2002, in need of a salary more than anything else, I joined Rapp Collins as CEO of the New York office. The challenge before me was daunting: five rounds of layoffs over the previous two years had left the shop decimated, demoralized, and fearful. The previous president had been fired a year before I arrived. In the interim, the agency's chairman did his best to run the office as acting chief, but his attention was needed elsewhere, and it showed. The agency continued to lose clients, money, and staff. If ever there was a doom loop, this was it.

I got down to business, only to face more setbacks, the results of problems that had been neglected for too long. I improved the work, recognized talented people who stayed, shored up restless clients. But even so, I met subversive resistance along the way from people who liked the agency the way it was and rebelled at change. There were very few happy moments in days punctuated with disappointment.

One of those happy moments was the publication of the first edition of *The Art of Client Service*. I was proud of writing something other than a proposal or a presentation, something that actually could prove useful to people. The book sold well, and I received encouraging emails from people who found it to be a bit of salvation.

Yet the book laid bare a serious problem. I offered a complimentary copy to anyone at the agency who would stop by my office for the book. With few exceptions, there were no takers. I knew I wasn't winning the popular vote—mostly because I had to fire people who clearly were not performing effectively—but this was a chilling condemnation.

In the spring of 2003, we found a way out of our continuing downturn through a major pitch that would involve most of the agency's U.S. offices. All we had to do was win.

Our chairman was leading the effort, but then he was forced to the sidelines by a serious illness. The agency turned to me. Against my better judgment, I assumed the lead. My reservations were well founded; it soon became clear that I wasn't what the client wanted in a leader.

It was a long, hard fight. But in the end, we lost the pitch.

And then I lost my job. After ten months leading an agency that I had no business even working for, I was out.

All of us know the five stages of grief: denial, anger, bargaining, depression, and acceptance. I wasn't quite able to manage that number. There were moments of anger and depression, but mostly I was relieved at the outcome. Being fired offered a chance to return to a business I knew and loved but somehow had lost sight of while trying to survive at an agency that didn't know what it meant to be great.

A couple of weeks later, I got a call from my former Ammirati colleagues Steve Gardner and Tom Nelson. They had been quietly building Gardner Nelson & Partners, and they saw a need and an opportunity to add direct marketing to their capabilities. Was I interested?

I didn't think twice. I had partnered with Steve and Tom when I was at Ammirati, and this was an opportunity to pick up where I'd left off.

I have been at Gardner Nelson & Partners ever since, first as a full-time staffer, more recently as a regular, retained consultant.

Most account people are very much in touch with what you might call "the law of unintended consequences." They know that anything they do might lead to unexpected results. And that is what happened with me in my new job.

I had previously headed three different agencies, and in each case, I was supported by a full complement of experts in media, in production, in creative, and of course, account management. In 1999, when I sat down to write and self-publish *Brain Surgery for Suits,* which would become *The Art of Client Service* in 2003, I could report on what I *believed* made a good account person. But I had limited firsthand experience.

When I arrived at Gardner Nelson, I had an opportunity to see if my opinions were true. I held the title of "managing partner," but I was actually a line account guy, responsible for every facet of bringing an idea to life. I was deeply involved in creative, media, and production. If there was a conference report to write, I wrote it. A schedule—the same. A budget—that, too. I spoke with and emailed clients every day. If there was a problem, it was mine to solve.

All of the things I talked about in the book, I now actually had to *do.*

Yesterday, I sat down and re-read the previous edition of *The Art of Client Service* cover to cover. And this is what I found to be true:

All of it.

Over the past four years, I had taken my own advice. I discovered that if you follow the principles outlined in this book, you will, in fact, have happier clients and well-supported colleagues. Most of the time, this approach will ensure more enduring relationships built on trust.

But as thorough as *The Art of Client Service* tried to be, a few things were missing. With this edition, I try to fill in the blanks.

The book starts with an introduction by David Verklin, CEO of media agency Carat Americas, published author, renowned speaker, and generally all-around nice guy. David knows the impact of consistent client service on an agency's bottom line and is a passionate advocate for making it a priority in his organization.

The new edition continues with a section that asks, "Does Advertising Matter?" Here, I suggest you don't need to be an account executive or to work in advertising to get something meaningful and rewarding from this book.

After that, I propose "Why Client Service Matters," in which I make the business case for why it is so important to have account people who truly care about the business, who are truly invested in its success.

Lots of new books have been published since I wrote the annotated bibliography that appears in Chapter 57. I still recommend all 15 of the books that I recommended in 2003, but there are 5 notable additions to the list as well.

In revisiting the book, what seemed to be missing was greater substance on communication. Although Chapter 6 included useful information on writing a creative brief, the previous edition was silent on the other forms of writing account people typically engage in, especially letters of proposal and PowerPoint presentations. That's why Chapter 44 is devoted to "How to Write a Letter of Proposal" and Chapter 45 decodes "The Zen of PowerPoint."

In recent years, technology has had a profound impact by enabling people to research practically anything, a phenomenon that I address in Chapter 46, "In a Hi-Tech World, Be Low-Tech."

I devote an entire section of the book to "Trouble," but I have a new and particularly embarrassing story to share, which I relate in Chapter 51, "What Happens When I Screw Up?"

Somewhere in this book, I point out that the difference between good creative work and great creative work can be the thinnest of margins and that the enemy of *great* is not *bad* but *good*. Having worked with clients day-to-day, I realize the same is true of client service: the enemy of *great* is *good*. Which is why, even if you are familiar with the previous edition of *The Art of Client Service,* I suggest that you revisit the chapters you read earlier. There is much worth remembering in those pages.

As I look back on *Brain Surgery for Suits* and the first edition of *The Art of Client Service,* I think of this current book as the third, and perhaps final, stage of learning what it really means to work at client service every day in a way that can make a difference. I'm hoping this time I got it a little more right.

In the introduction to the previous edition of *The Art of Client Service,* I talked about William Strunk and E. B. White's *The Elements of Style* and how I hoped that my book someday would be viewed in a similar light. This edition shares with its predecessors a focus on the fundamentals that define outstanding client service. If it helps you solve even just one problem or teaches you just one new idea or technique, then it will have served its purpose well.

If not, it's comforting that the book's brevity, levity, and clarity make for fast and relatively painless reading. And failing that, at least the cartoons are funny.

Does Advertising Matter?

Well, it does to me. But as I was rereading this book, I wasn't thinking about advertising. I thought about my two bankers.

One is a large, well-known investment firm with a long-term track record of success. The other is a small firm that isn't nearly as well known (calling them a "boutique" confers more stature than is deserved) with a much shorter track record (more impressive if stated in months, not years). For business reasons, I recently felt the need to consolidate with one of the two banks.

Both banks performed well, with the larger bank performing better overall. Logic would dictate I go with the larger firm; at minimum, it would be much easier to justify in cocktail party chatter. But for some reason, I hesitated.

One reason was that the larger bank had changed my rep three times in four years. The first time they made a switch, they invited me to a meeting and made a bit of a show to gain my buy-in, which I read as a way to keep me from bolting with the banker who'd just left. But at least they made an effort.

The second time they made a little less of a show. No meeting—instead they sent a letter. Shortly thereafter, I met my new rep; he sounded like a broker disguised as a banker. In our first meeting, I talked about liquidating some assets to take advantage of a real estate opportunity. In response, my new banker/broker reminded me of the bank's minimum investment threshold. That made me feel right at home.

Later, when I wanted to move some assets to cash, I felt strangely guilty. In fact, every time I asked for money, I felt as though I was asking my dad for my allowance, only my banker was a good bit younger than me.

In contrast, when I spoke to the smaller bank, they always seemed more relaxed and whole lot less judgmental. When asked, they offered good advice. When I had a question about a transaction, I could quickly get one of the partners on the phone to talk about it. Service was never an issue; it felt as though they wanted to keep my business. The bigger bank? I wasn't so sure.

I let the smaller bank know that I was considering a consolidation. They responded thoughtfully and without pressure. Let us know, they said; we'd be happy to help if we can. After many weeks of hand-wringing, I made a decision, which in reality was no decision at all. I chose the smaller bank.

After some protestations that betrayed a lack of graciousness, the banker at the bigger firm simply gave up. He made little effort to discover the reasons for my departure, which made me think it didn't really matter much and served to validate my choice.

Had this been a performance issue, my decision would have gone the other way. The bigger bank performed better. But it wasn't about performance; it was about service. And this made me think about *The Art of Client Service.* Everything the smaller bank did right is contained in the pages of this book.

A good friend of mine—also an investment banker, I should add—reinforced this sentiment. "We live in a service economy," he said. "Everyone can benefit from *The Art of Client Service.*" He's right, of course.

Elsewhere in this book, I recommend Malcolm Gladwell's *Blink.* On pages 40–41 of his book, Gladwell talked about the doctor–patient relationship:

> Believe it or not, the risk of being sued for malpractice has very little to do with how many mistakes a doctor makes. Analyses of malpractice lawsuits show that there are highly skilled doctors who get sued a lot and doctors who make lots of mistakes and never get sued. . . . In other words, patients don't file lawsuits because they've been harmed by shoddy medical care. Patients file lawsuits because they've been harmed by shoddy medical care and *something else* happens to them.
>
> "What is that something else? It's how they were treated by their doctor. . . . It isn't necessary, then, to know much about how a surgeon operates in order to know his likelihood of being sued. What you need to understand is the relationship between the doctor and his patients.

There's more to Gladwell's doctor story than appears here, so I urge you to read the book. But his point is that relationships matter more than technical expertise.

The Art of Client Service will be helpful if you're a doctor, a lawyer, a banker, an accountant, a financial advisor, a consultant, an architect, a sales rep, or anyone else who cares about the relationship you forge with clients. Virtually all the lessons I draw on from my failures will be relevant and meaningful to you.

Even though advertising is important to me and I strive to do it better every day, you need not care at all about it to gain something useful from this book.

Why Client Service Matters

If you are in advertising, you know that the only thing that really matters is the work.

Great work makes everyone want to be a part of the agency. Great work commands a price premium. Great work wins business.

It's no surprise that most agency people figure that if they do great work, everything else will take care of itself, including the relationships they build with clients. When I joined the advertising business, that's pretty much what I thought.

There's just one problem with this assumption: it's wrong.

Great work does not shield you or your agency from client loss. You can do great work and still get fired.

My former agency, Ammirati and Puris, did great work

for BMW. The agency wrote the line, "the ultimate driving machine," which endures to this day. BMW kept the line, but they didn't keep the agency.

Ammirati and Puris is not alone. TBWA/Chiat Day did great work for Taco Bell. It's no longer Taco Bell's agency. Deutch did great work for Ikea. It's no longer working with Ikea. BBDO did great work for Charles Schwab. It's no longer Schwab's agency.

You can make your own list; it probably will be longer than mine. So what went wrong? We know it wasn't the work. The work was great.

Then I thought about all the agencies whose work fell short of the mark yet somehow managed to hold onto the business. One of the best examples is Fallon and United Airlines.

After Fallon won the United business, it launched the "Rising" campaign. Wrong message, wrong time. People knew travel was hell; they were tired of the empty promises most airlines made. Yet the "Rising" ads clung to notions of romanticism that every savvy traveler knew to be false.

Not surprisingly, the campaign met uniform criticism. Fallon is a terrific agency, but this was bad advertising.

So bad, in fact, that you would think United would have gone searching for another agency. But they didn't. They stayed with Fallon until Fallon got it right.

Why was that? One report claimed that the close personal relationship between Pat Fallon and United's chairman kept the agency in good graces, even when its work was far from stellar.

What went right? We know that it wasn't the work.

I used to think that great work would lead to a great relationship. Now I think the opposite: a great relationship leads to great work. The reason is pretty simple.

Great work entails risk. Most clients do not want to take risks; they prefer a safe retreat into the world of the merely good or, worse, the dismissively average. Still, if they are going to take that risk, they are much more likely to do so with agency people they trust. And trust is the very foundation of a great relationship. And that's why I say a great relationship leads to great work. Think of it as a perfect three-legged stool:

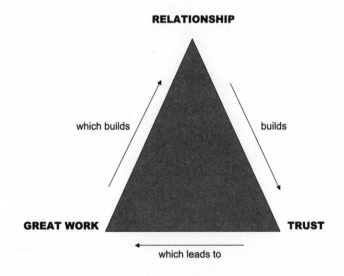

RELATIONSHIP

which builds

builds

GREAT WORK

TRUST

which leads to

Some of what follows is about working with agency colleagues, but most is about building trust with clients.

And this, in the end, is why client service matters. It matters because the work matters. And creating great work is what drives and inspires all of us every day.

PART ONE

The Work

"I just have a few minor fixes that will ruin everything you've come up with."

CHAPTER 1

Define Success

A client calls with an assignment. As usual, the deadline is tight. You spring into action, gathering background material, organizing a team, developing a budget and a schedule.

In that initial frenzy of activity, don't forget to ask your client, "What do you want this advertising to do?" It seems so obvious, and yet it's so easy to overlook.

You need to begin every client relationship, and every client advertising effort, with a clear understanding of what the client wants to achieve. Be sure to ask about the business goals, the sales goals, and the communication goals. Ask about the response the client wants from the key constituencies: customers, prospects, employees, company management, shareholders, the press, and the competition.

I'm all for clients having lofty aspirations, and for pushing agencies to achieve them, but you should encourage your clients to set goals that are in line with reality. On more than one occasion my clients have set objectives that were all but impossible to achieve. A situation like this can turn success into failure, where the problem isn't that the advertising fell short, but that the goal was too tall. This is something to discuss, and agree on, at the outset. This is not something you want to argue about after the fact.

When it comes to goal setting, you should pay attention not just to your clients' *company* goals, but also to their *personal* goals. Most of the clients I know are ambitious; they want to achieve success for their companies, as well as advance in their careers. Usually the company and personal goals are aligned and mutually beneficial. Occasionally these goals are in conflict.

A client might be more concerned about protecting personal turf and power than collaborating with other departments to accomplish bigger and better things. A client might be so fearful of making a mistake, so intolerant of risk, that the agency is unable to do anything but average, safe work.

Personal agendas like these—sometimes hidden, sometimes quite apparent—can undermine your ability to do the best possible advertising. You must be aware of them, and take them into account when you sit down to define success at the start of a relationship or a project. It can be a balancing act, but remember that your first duty is to deliver on the clients' *company* goals.

I once went a little off course when it came to setting a goal for a particular ad campaign. My agency was creating some advertising for a client I knew well. I thought the advertising could achieve one result; he thought it could achieve a much higher result. In a moment of misplaced certitude, I offered to make a little wager on the outcome of the campaign. My client was a clothes-horse, so I suggested the loser take the winner to a certain very exclusive men's store and buy the winner one item of his choosing. With a smile and a laugh, he took the bet.

I was sure I would win, and figured I'd pick a pair of socks or something equally inexpensive. I didn't think my client had a prayer of winning.

It turns out the advertising achieved a result far greater than even my client predicted. A very happy problem to have. Because my client's estimate was much closer to being right than mine, it was time to take him shopping.

My client was very gracious. He could have picked a new suit; he could have picked a new coat. Instead, he chose a tie, and thereby let me off the hook. Every time I saw him in that tie, though, he would say, "Want to make a wager? I need a nice suit to go with this tie." It was our private joke.

There's no moral to this story except to say, define success at the outset, but don't bet on it.

CHAPTER **2**

Be Multilingual

There's an old saying, "If the only tool you have is a hammer, every problem looks like a nail." For advertising agencies, the hammer has been television, and it can make every problem look like one to be solved with a 30-second broadcast television spot. Sure there's radio, print, and outdoor, but the biggest tool by far in the agency toolbox is network television.

These days, network TV isn't quite the hammer it once was. First came cable. Then the Web. In recent years we've seen the rise of guerrilla marketing techniques and the power of product placement. Clients are investing more money in promotion, sponsorships, trade shows, and proprietary meetings and events. Then there's direct marketing, relationship marketing, and customer relationship management (CRM).

In a world of ever-expanding marketing choices and fragmenting markets, you need to be multilingual if you are going to provide your client good counsel. You've got to speak not only brand advertising, but also every other discipline and medium available to your clients. That requires you to learn enough about each marketing discipline and media option so that you can recommend the combination that will achieve the best results at the most efficient cost.

You don't need to become completely fluent in every marketing language; there are native speakers in every discipline and medium you can call on for help. The key is to be thinking about the best combination of marketing disciplines and media options to meet your client's needs, not about the next big TV campaign.

The advertising business refers to this as being discipline and media "agnostic." I take a slightly different view. I call it being deeply religious—about delivering what's right for your client.

CHAPTER 3

Live the Client's Brand

Years ago I worked for an agency that was one of three sharing a major financial services account. The client decided to consolidate its work with one shop, and invited all three incumbents to pitch for the business. I led the team representing my agency.

The shop I worked for was young, a little light on reputation, and very short on capabilities. We couldn't begin to equal the depth of resources of our competitors. The two other incumbents were bigger, better known, and better connected with the client.

We knew we were overmatched, but instead of being intimidated, we used our underdog status as motivation. We already knew the client's business, having worked on it for more than a year. But we acted as if we didn't, and went "back to school" on the whole industry. We dug deeply into issues and worked relentlessly to uncover insights that would help the client grow its business. We invested time in understanding what each person on the client team expected from its agency, and we made a strong final presentation.

To everyone's surprise, we were the client's choice. It was a big win for us.

Sometime later, after having gotten to know our lead client, I felt comfortable enough to ask him about the pitch and why we won.

"All the agencies were good—any of the three could have done the job for us," he said. "What really impressed us about your shop was how you spoke our language. You sounded like one of us. You demonstrated that you knew what we were about. The other agencies didn't appear to be as comfortable or as confident. That made an impact."

It made an impact on me too. It goes without saying that you should be a customer of your client. (If, as David Ogilvy has written, he found a way to buy all his clothes at Sears after his agency won that account, you can find a way to use your clients' products too.) But you need to go beyond that. You've got to steep yourself in the client's brand. Here's what I mean.

- Know the history of the company. Know the people who work there. Observe the culture.

- Talk with other people who buy the brand. Ask them why.

- Read what the press says. Understand what Wall Street thinks. Pay attention to opinion leaders.

- Form a point of view on the company and the brand's strengths, weaknesses, opportunities, and threats.

- Always be open to, and seek out, new sources of information and insight. Think about the new ways your client can address a problem or capitalize on an opportunity. Present those thoughts whenever appropriate and in whatever form and forum are most effective for your client.

At many companies, product and marketing managers come and go. When new clients come in, their first instinct often is to put the account in review. Your years of knowledge can help counter that impulse. You can be an invaluable source of history and continuity for new clients. You can help them get up to speed quickly and be more effective in their jobs. In so doing, you can help keep the account right where it is, at your agency.

Just one more reason to live the client's brand.

CHAPTER 4

Agree on a Strategy, a Budget, and a Schedule

My client, Leslie, called in a near-panic. "The product group wants to announce a new promotion in *USA Today* and *The New York Times*," she said.

"Good," I replied.

"Not good," she said, "They want the ad to run this Friday."

"Not good," I agreed. "Why Friday?"

"To drive traffic to the stores this weekend," she answered.

"Look, we're used to turning around advertising in a matter of days," I said, "but it's Wednesday and there's no way to create anything even halfway respectable when we've got maybe 24 hours to do it. They should have come to you sooner. What about next Friday?"

"I already tried that with the product group. They were immovable. They said next Friday is not an option. So we've got to do this; I don't have a choice, and neither do you."

"What if we both spoke to them?" I suggested. "Maybe I could convince them this is a blueprint for disaster. I'll take the heat, instead of you."

There was silence at the other end of the phone. Finally, Leslie said, "I already told them we could do it."

It took every ounce of self-control to keep from shouting, "You told them yes! You know it's insane to do this! Couldn't you at least check with us first?"

But I knew that would only make the situation worse. Instead, I simply said, "Give me an hour. I'll call you back." I hung up the phone and went to work.

I gathered a team and briefed them on the call. First there was disbelief, followed by a bit of hysterical laughter, which quickly escalated into full-blown rage. After 15 minutes of venting—at the client, at me—the group weighed the trade-offs. We could refuse to do the work; we certainly would have been right. The client knew we weren't set up to do quick-turn retail advertising.

But refusing could cost us the account. Was there a way to pull this off?

There was. We could build the ad based on a format we had used before. We could get briefed by the client, and come back later in the afternoon with a couple of headline ideas. The client would choose one, we'd write copy and do a layout that night, send a comp to the client in the morning, get sign-off with minimal changes, go right to finished art, then transmit the finished files to the newspapers. There'd be no creative brief, no usual rounds of concepting, no face-to-face presentation, and no usual rounds of refinement, proofing, and quality control. It was possible. God knows what kind of advertising would come out of this effort, but we were willing to try. People decided to take it as a challenge. "Advertising on speed," one of the writers called it.

I called the client. "Leslie, here's what we can do," I said. I outlined the plan, and told her what she'd have to do to make it work. She agreed to the schedule.

So we were briefed by the client product group. The writers came up with not two, but three pretty clever headlines. We slapped them into layouts and sent these to the client. They selected one on the spot.

That evening we worked on the copy and tightened the layout. By midnight, we sent them to the client and called it a day. We were scheduled to speak with the client at 8:00 the following morning.

That's when things began to unravel. The client delayed our conference call two hours, costing us time when we had none to spare. When we finally spoke at 10:00, we expected the client to give us the go-ahead, with maybe a minor change or two. How silly of us.

The client had extensive copy changes. That was an additional setback, but the writers took it in stride and turned around the copy by early afternoon. The client approved the revision.

Then we had to scramble to get the finished ad to the newspapers. There wasn't enough time for the normal rounds of proofing, but we made the Thursday evening deadline. We were pretty proud of ourselves. We enjoyed the moment—but it didn't last.

The ad ran as scheduled. Except for the typographical error, it looked pretty good.

We couldn't believe we'd missed it. It was there, plain as day. The error didn't affect the content of the ad. It was not as if we got the name of the product wrong, or ran an incorrect price. Still, it was enough to make all of us want to weep. We had worked incredibly hard. But we screwed up.

The client was looking at the ad when I called. "How could this happen?" Leslie asked.

"How could it not," I replied. "We're mortified, and very, very sorry. Because we were running so fast, and had so little time, we didn't see a final proof."

She ignored me. "The product group is pretty upset, and so am I. I look bad, you look bad, the whole thing is disaster. And my boss wants you to eat the cost of the ad."

My answer was measured, but I didn't hesitate, "I'll talk to your boss, and I'll explain why we're not going to do that. I'll also write you a letter detailing what happened and why."

"And why is it that you're not willing to pay for the ad?" Leslie asked, her voice just ever so slightly louder.

"Three reasons," I responded. "First, we would have caught the error had we seen a final proof. The only reason we didn't have time for the proof is because you delayed our 8:00 AM meeting to 10:00 AM. Those lost two hours cost us that opportunity. Second, the error occurred when we made the major copy revisions you gave us. We had agreed there would be only minor changes, not massive ones. Third, the mistake doesn't affect the content of the promotion. It's a stupid mistake, but not a fatal one. It's not as if we got a product name wrong, or a price wrong."

All Leslie said before hanging up was, "I'll wait for your letter."

She had it later that day. In it I apologized again for the mistake, and meticulously reconstructed how it happened. I also pointed out that if our clients refuse to adhere to the steps we use to ensure the work is done right, and the work comes out wrong, the agency surely shouldn't have to pay for it.

After some back and forth on the phone with Leslie, with her boss, and with the product group, the client grudgingly conceded the agency wasn't truly at fault, and did not ask us to pay for the ad. We had a long history with this client before doing what became known as the McAd disaster, and I'm glad to say we had a long history after. We even did a few more McAds, but we insisted the client agree up front that if there were a mistake, the agency was not financially liable.

So what's the point of this too-long story? The point is: In a world where every client wants it yesterday and every assignment is a rush job, it is tempting to take shortcuts. Forget the budget. Forget the schedule. Who needs a strategy? We'll just wing it.

You've got to start every assignment with a budget, a schedule, and a brief that your client buys into. Then you've got to do everything you can to maintain the integrity of those items as the assignment progresses.

If you don't, if you subvert the very processes that help you and your colleagues get it right the *first* time, you surely will find yourselves working to get it right the *second* time. As the saying goes, "There is always time to do it over."

CHAPTER 5

Always Manage
Client Expectations
from the Outset

A creative director and I were presenting some concepts for a print ad to a client we really liked. Although this client had limited experience working with agencies and evaluating creative, he was smart, knew what he wanted, and respected our work.

We presented three ideas. The client responded positively to all of them, but was absolutely passionate about one particular approach, which relied on an illustration for the visual.

The creative director, who was also an art director, had done a little sketch of the idea he had in mind for the illustration. The client positively loved that sketch. "It's the perfect payoff to the headline," he said. "It's witty and charming." The creative director also had brought along examples of the work of the illustrator he wanted to use to execute the sketch. He showed the examples to the client.

The client wasn't wild about the illustrator, and he had a pained expression when we told him the cost. Still he said, "You're the experts. If you say she's the right person to do the job, let's spend the money and go with her."

This story should have a happy ending, but it doesn't. The client was bitterly disappointed with the finished ad. To him, something was lost in the translation between concept and execution. "This just doesn't work for me," he said. "It was great when you first showed it to me, but the finished ad just doesn't work as well as I thought it would." It was especially painful to him that he had spent thousands of dollars on an illustration he didn't like. "I wish we had just used the sketch instead," he lamented.

I don't blame the illustrator; she executed the direction the creative director gave her. I don't blame the creative director; he thought he had buy-in from the client on both the concept and the choice of illustrator. He was mystified by the client's disappointment. I certainly don't blame the client, who was very supportive of what we were trying to deliver.

I blame me.

I did two things wrong: First, I missed the client's signals about his lack of full endorsement of the choice of illustrator and the associated cost. Second, I didn't manage the client's expectations about what the finished illustration would look like, and how it would differ from the creative director's sketch.

When the client hesitated about the illustrator, I should have said to the creative director, "Tony, can you explain how your sketch will translate into the finished visual?" After Tony explained, I should have turned to my client and said, "Are you okay with this? Have we been clear on how the illustration will not look exactly like the sketch?" Had I initiated that conversation, had I drawn the client out, it would have revealed the client's concerns. Then we either would have satisfied those concerns and managed the client's expectations, or we would have concluded we needed to find another way to execute the sketch into a finished illustration. We likely would have avoided the client's unhappiness.

That one incident had repercussions beyond the print ad. The client never again trusted us quite the way he once did. We had a harder time getting him to buy work. He became more risk adverse. I'd even go so far as to say the quality of work suffered.

That was a long time ago. These days, thanks to computer technology, agencies generally present initial creative concepts in such finished form they look like final ads. But the problem remains the same as before: If you don't manage the client's expectations, the client will take the concepts literally. Unless you explain otherwise, clients buy exactly what they see, which can limit the agency's ability to evolve the work to a better place.

So the lesson is, manage your client expectations from the outset. Make sure your clients understand how you and your colleagues approach a given assignment: What the steps are. What the agency will deliver at each step. When they will see the work, and in what form. How to interpret the storyboard or comp. Who will present the work, and where you would like to conduct the meeting.

Listen carefully for client concerns, even when they are not stated overtly. Especially when they are not stated overtly. Ask questions. Probe for answers. Draw the client out.

I missed a subtle signal that, in retrospect, was quite clear. If you observe and listen to your client, you can do better than I did.

CHAPTER 6

Take the Word *Brief* Seriously

I once worked at an agency where we wrote briefs that were as fat as the Manhattan Yellow Pages (well, maybe not quite that big, but you get the picture). The account guys wrote them (there were no planners at this shop). We were so proud of these briefs. They were so thorough, so exhaustive in their detail, so exhausting to read.

The agency hired a new creative director, who tried working with these briefs for a few months. One day he appeared in the doorway of my office, my latest masterwork in hand (actually in two hands; it was a two-fisted document). His expression was a combination of exasperation and despair. "This isn't a brief; it's the anti-brief!" he exclaimed.

He sat down and dropped the offending document on my desk. It landed with a solid thud. "Here's what we need," he said, as he pulled out a pen and scribbled this outline:

1. Key fact

2. Problem

3. Objective

4. Key benefit

5. Support

6. Tone

7. Audience

8. Competition

9. Mandatories

"That's it," he said. "Forget about telling me every-thing you know; just tell me what I need to know in order to make good advertising." Before he stomped out, he added, "And stop writing these things on your own. Get the creatives in the room with you and figure it out together."

Now, this creative director could have gone to any number of account people at the agency, but he came to me. I didn't know whether to be flattered or insulted, but I guess he chose me because I wrote the longest briefs of all. I'd also like to think it was because he saw there was hope for me.

I resisted at first, but ultimately did what he asked. To my astonishment, he was right. Our briefs became sharper, tighter, and more focused. The whole creative process became sharper, tighter, and more focused. The creative work that came out of those briefs was sharper, tighter, and more focused. Better still, instead of confining the work, the tighter briefs had the opposite impact. They had a liberating effect on our writers and art directors, who now felt free to explore widely in and around the direction provided in the brief.

Initially, it was a struggle to get creative people to attend sessions where we would work on the brief together. But ultimately, the whole agency adopted the new format for the brief, and the collaborative process for writing it, as the basis for creating work. In fact, the creative staff became so committed to the process that they would refuse to work on an assignment unless there was at least one session in which they participated in the development of the brief.

The version of the brief we actually adopted was not as clipped as the one the creative director wrote out in my office, but it remained very tight.

Using a form like the one on the next page, we created briefs that were always just one or two pages. It led to some consistently excellent advertising.

There probably are as many different kinds of briefs as there are agencies. And with the rise of account planning, the development of creative briefs has taken on new dimensions since the days my agency first deployed the form below. So I'm not suggesting this is the definitive brief format and that you should promptly abandon whatever your agency is currently using.

What I am suggesting is that you take the word *brief* seriously. There is a saying: "I didn't have time to write you a short letter, so I wrote you a long one." That says it all.

CREATIVE STRATEGY
Account Name
Specific Assignment Name
Job Number
Date

Key fact
A one- or two-sentence distillation of the current consumer marketing situation or environment.

What consumer problem must the advertising solve?
A precise definition, written from the consumer perspective, *not* the client perspective.

What is the objective of the advertising?
This flows from the definition of the consumer problem.

What is the most important benefit, promise, and/or offer?
Must be strong enough to overcome the problem and meet the objective.

What facts support this benefit, promise, and/or offer?
Should be a simple listing; if additonal information is needed, provide as an attachment.

Who are we talking to?
Provide psychographics, in addition to demographics, to the extent they are known or can be intuited.

Who or what are we competing with?
Products and services, as well as companies and internal competitors, if there are any.

What should the tone of the advertising be?
Describe with a series of adjectives. Be as specific, concrete, and evocative as possible.

Are there any mandatories we must account for in the advertising?
Is there anything we must deal with, officially (such as logo size/placement) or unofficially (such as client preferences)?

Approvals:

Account _____

Creative _____

Client _____

Brevity is hard work. The key to achieving it lies not in the initial writing, but in rewriting, rewriting, and rewriting, to distill the brief to its essence. There should be no wasted words.

Brevity is crucial because a brief that isn't brief is no help to anyone. The reader can't distinguish the important points from the underbrush of detail in which they are hidden. The client won't embrace it, the creative team won't follow it, and the work will suffer because of it.

A good brief is critical to achieving great creative work. And a good brief *is* brief.

CHAPTER 7

Know When to Look It Up;
Know When to Make It Up

I was working with some colleagues on an advertising assignment for Myers's rum. We were struggling with the rum's dark color. "People think of rum as being clear," said one of my colleagues. "I don't know," I said, "I don't think rum is supposed to be clear. The way I see it, Myers's is the color of rum." One of my colleagues replied, "That's it! That's the line: Myers's *is* the color of rum." We used it in our advertising. Our client loved it.

Another time, this same group of colleagues and I struggled to devise a name for a customer loyalty program we were developing for Polaroid. The reward for using Polaroid cameras and film was going to be frequent flyer mileage. We didn't know what to call it. Out of the blue one of my colleagues said, "Let's call it the *Polaroid Frequent Smileage Program.*" We loved it, the client loved it, and that's what we named the program.

Recently I was sitting around at a conference room table, surrounded by a sea of paper, working with a colleague on a brand positioning assignment for a client. We were early on in the process; we hadn't even completed our research. But we were talking about finding a positioning the client could own, one that would speak to the company's strengths and would energize its employees.

We took a break. While sitting there, three words came into my head. When we reconvened, I told my colleague, "I have an idea. I don't know if it's worth a damn or not, but let me try it on you." I wrote the three words on a sheet of paper and held it up. "What do you think?" I asked. "Does it work?"

It did indeed work. It was a creative leap, right past the positioning to a tagline. All our work to date validated those three words. We would have to see if it held up. If it did, we knew what our positioning recommendation would be.

You can spend weeks, even months, immersed in research, but insights often come in a flash of recognition.

One clear insight is worth a thousand data points. Of course, you need to do the heavy lifting in the marketplace—the customer research, the competitive analysis, the field visits—but there comes a time when you should put the research away and go with your instinct. Sometimes too much data can interfere with understanding. The secret is to combine what you know with what you feel in order to push for new ideas and better solutions.

If you can do that, you have a future in account management.

CHAPTER 8

Make the Creative Team
Partners in the Brief

Martin Puris, cofounder of Ammirati & Puris, where I once worked, used to say that 80 percent of all creative work fails before one word of copy is written. That's because if the strategy is wrong, there is little hope of getting the advertising right.

So how do you get the strategy right? Certainly not by sitting in your office alone, banging out the strategy brief in isolation. Even if your agency has an account planning department, and the planners are responsible for leading creative strategy development, you don't want them writing the brief on their own.

You get the strategy right by recognizing that developing the strategy is a team sport, and the creative crew—the writer and art director assigned to work on the ad or the campaign—are critical team members. You shouldn't just hand them a brief, you should work with them to create the brief.

There are three reasons to do this.

1. It helps the creative team become immersed in the assignment and take ownership of it. The creative team's active participation ensures that the brief that emerges from the development process actually will assist in the creation of effective advertising.

2. The creative team will help unearth issues or gaps in knowledge, which gives you an early opportunity to address the issues or fill the knowledge gaps.

3. The creative team will help uncover insights or help make connections that otherwise might be missed. Writers and art directors generally see things from a perspective different from yours. You want to capture that perspective early on in the creative process, during the development of the brief that will drive the work.

Thinking about what Martin Puris said, I'm reminded that there's one other reason to involve the creative team: to ensure that the advertising that results is among the 20 percent that succeeds, not the 80 percent that fails.

CHAPTER 9

In Writing the Brief, Provide the Client's Perspective

One of your key roles is to represent the client within the agency to your colleagues. In fact, no one in your agency should know the client better than you do. You want to be the first person that agency staffers turn to when they want to know something about your client.

That means making yourself an expert on your client's products, people, and culture. Here's how to do that.

- *Spend as much time in your client's offices as you do your own.* It's amazing how much you can learn by walking the halls, eating in the cafeteria, and generally seeing first-hand how the company works.

- *Get out in the field.* Nothing is more valuable than meeting your client's customers and hearing their issues and concerns. Traveling with the salespeople who serve those customers gives you an opportunity to get their frontline perspective on the company, its customers, and its competitors.

- *Spend time with your clients away from the office.* If I have a meeting scheduled with an out-of-town client, I make it a point to arrive the evening before. I schedule a dinner for that evening with one of my key client contacts. I schedule a breakfast the following morning with a different client contact. I'll have lunch that day with yet a third client contact. My purpose isn't to run up a big entertainment bill. My purpose is to use that time away from the client's office not only to talk business, but also to really get to know my clients, to understand their professional and personal goals. I also use that time to uncover any issues and concerns with the agency and its work that might not be readily visible. It's not that I learn *more* things in these out-of-the-office sessions with clients, I learn *different* things.

- *Read the trades.* Virtually every industry has publications that cover the field. You should become a subscriber and a regular reader. While we're on the subject of reading, you should not only read your client's annual report, you should regularly visit the company's Web site to check for the latest product announcements, news releases, white papers, speeches, and other materials.

- *Watch the competition.* You should gather everything you can on the competition: advertising, articles, speeches by management, Wall Street analyst reports, and anything else that's available. At least twice a year, you should provide a synthesis and an analysis of the competitive landscape, for the benefit of both your client and your colleagues on the account.

- *Be a customer.* You should buy the products and services your client sells. The purchasing process can be telling. By using the product or service, by being a customer, you can better understand what other customers experience.

Doing these things gives you a perspective that can help sharpen and define the marketing and creative strategy the agency develops to drive creative work. It also can help uncover the overlooked fact that may drive an insight that results in killer advertising.

Here's an example of what I mean. Back in the 1980s, Ammirati & Puris created a wonderful advertising campaign for UPS. The tagline for the campaign was "We run the tightest ship in the shipping business." One of the commercials in that award-winning campaign was called "Washing Planes." It explained that the frequent washing of planes helped reduce air drag, which in turn reduced fuel consumption, which in turn helped UPS be more efficient and thus allowed the company to charge lower prices for overnight delivery than Federal Express.

How did the agency discover that washing planes makes them more efficient in air? It's not as if someone at UPS said, "Hey let's make a commercial about how clean we keep our planes." Instead, it came from the agency team immersing itself in the UPS culture. That little-known fact became the basis of a smart, engaging, and memorable commercial that delivered big impact.

CHAPTER 10

Get the Client's Input and Approval on the Brief

There's an illness in the advertising world that occasionally afflicts a client. I call it *brief amnesia*. It's not amnesia that lasts a short duration. It's amnesia about approving a creative brief.

Here's how the illness strikes.

You send a creative brief to your client for approval. The client, up to her eyeballs in work, gives the brief the once over. When you follow up with a call to see if the client has changes or input, the client says, "Looks good to me; let's go with it."

The creative team develops ad concepts based on the brief. You and the creative team present them to the client. The client rejects the work. You ask why. The client gives a reason that has nothing to do with the creative brief. You respond that the work is on strategy. The client barely remembers the strategy, let alone that she approved it. If she does remember, she doesn't care. Instead, she uses the concepts in front of her to re-engineer the strategy. You and your colleagues return to the agency. You start over from the beginning, developing a new brief.

That's brief amnesia at work.

So how do you inoculate your client against this dreadful disease? There's only one way: Make the client part of the process of developing the creative brief.

Here's what to do: Make sure the client does a full-scale download at the start of the assignment. Ideally, this takes place in a face-to-face meeting, but schedules being what they are, if you have to do it in a conference call, so be it.

What you're looking for from your client is 1) a clear statement of what the client wants to accomplish with the advertising, 2) all the facts related to the product or service that is the subject of the advertising, and 3) any mandatories the agency must take into account in developing the advertising.

Armed with this information, develop the brief. Once you and the team are satisfied with it, don't send it to the client. Take it to the client, and take him through it. Extract any additional input from him. Be alert to any concerns that arise. Go back and revise the brief if necessary, but make sure that the client is completely clear and completely comfortable with the brief.

Then make him sign it.

It's amazing how this simple act will make a client take notice. It says, "I'm taking ownership of this, I approve it, and I understand that my advertising will be based on it."

That's how you cure brief amnesia.

This is critical not only because the brief will guide creative development, but also because the brief serves as a yardstick by which to measure the concepts that emerge from it. You and your colleagues will use the brief to evaluate creative concepts before you show them to the client. You will make sure that each concept reflects the brief and is on strategy.

Then, when you present creative work to the client, it's a whole lot less likely that she'll use the work to reinvent the strategy.

What if there's a really great concept the creative team comes up with, but it's not on strategy? You explain to the client, "During creative development, we came up with another idea. We were going to discard it because it's clearly not on strategy. But we decided not to, because it's pretty compelling. We thought we'd show it to you."

Then you show it. If the client loves it, you'll have an interesting conversation and a decision to make. If the client doesn't love it, no problem. You've already presented great ideas that are on strategy.

The most important thing to remember is that to avoid brief amnesia, and to preempt clients from using the concept presentation to reinvent the strategy, make your client a partner in the development of the brief.

CHAPTER 11

Ask, "What Do My Colleagues Need to Create Great Advertising?" Then Deliver It

Tom Nelson, the cofounder and creative director of Gardner Nelson & Partners, says, "In my experience, account people spend too much time talking about partnership and not enough time practicing it. For your creative team, a detailed 16-point memo after the big presentation is no substitute for a lukewarm quart of Szechuan noodles the night before."

Tom is right. Many account people think the best way to help your colleagues is to be a resource to them. That's important, but the best account people go beyond being the repository of market and competitive wisdom. They go beyond being the expert on client wishes, requirements, and idiosyncrasies. They are a constant, contributing presence on every assignment.

If the creative team is working late, or working the weekend to make a deadline, great account people will be there with them. They are there to answer questions, to provide input, to offer feedback and encouragement, and to order Chinese food or pizza. They are there in solidarity with their colleagues, participating and contributing to the process in every way that's helpful.

Often it is the smallest gesture that makes the biggest impact. I remember a particularly stressful time preparing for a new business presentation. It was late on a Friday evening; most of the agency staff had called it a day. But one of my colleagues who was working on the pitch with me, a planner, was struggling to make the final revisions to the creative brief. She wasn't the most proficient person at the keyboard. I volunteered to help.

We sat in my office and worked from her rough notes. She dictated; I keyed. In an hour we had input the revisions and had the final version ready for distribution to the creative team.

It wasn't a big thing; maybe I saved the planner a half hour. But I know it made a difference, because the planner thanked me more than once. To this day we are friends, and on occasion she will remind me of that Friday evening. "You have no idea how important that was," she'll say. "You were a big help at a difficult moment."

She wasn't thanking me for my typing skills. She was thanking me for my gesture of support. It was almost as good as that quart of lukewarm Szechuan noodles Tom Nelson talks about.

By the way, I was at the agency early the following Saturday morning, to be available to the creative team. If I recall correctly, I brought bagels and coffee.

CHAPTER 12

Always Ask, "Does This Advertising Pass the 'So What' Test?"

The airwaves are filled with ads that, at best, put the viewer to sleep. At worst, they debase the client's brand, rather than build it.

It is not enough for the work to be on strategy; it has to engage consumers and make them want to pay attention. You can't influence how people think and act with boring advertising. To achieve those results requires advertising driven by a smart, honest, and emotionally true idea.

Whenever you're reviewing work with your creative colleagues, first ask yourself if it is on strategy. Then ask yourself if it makes you think, "So what?"

If the work doesn't pass this test, it will not pass the test of the marketplace. This isn't work that should go to the client. It is better, instead, to keep working, and to keep pushing for a solution that passes the "So what" test.

CHAPTER 13

Don't Fall in Love
with Good Work

There were safer alternatives on the wall, but my creative colleagues and I were convinced that one particular concept was right for the client. We were, however, having trouble convincing our boss, the head of the agency. We must have argued for an hour. He wanted to kill the idea; we wanted to make it our recommendation.

We took a break. The boss and I had a little conversation on our own.

"We can't go with that campaign as the recommendation," he said. "It's too risky and the client will never buy it."

"It is risky," I conceded, "but not because it's wrong, or because it's off strategy. It's risky because the client has never seen anything like this from us before, and it's not what she's expecting. We'd be crazy to kill it without at least showing it to her. It's just too good."

"But I really don't like it," my boss persisted.

"But all of us do," I countered. "If it were off strategy, I'd agree with you, but it isn't. It delivers perfectly on the strategy. It's brilliant and funny. There's a real idea at work. And it will have legs."

"I still don't like it." I could hear the frustration in his voice, but I wasn't going to give in.

"Look, do you really want to overrule me, the creative director, the writer, and the art director? It's four against one."

"Since when are all votes created equal?" he replied testily.

"Since never," I conceded. "But you yourself said it's my account to run. I'm asking you to trust my judgment. I know this client better than you do. They will love this work, and they're going to buy it."

"That's what I'm afraid of!" my boss exclaimed.

In the end, he backed off, grudgingly, reluctantly, fearfully. We could present the idea we were so in love with, but we also agreed to present four concepts instead of three, so the client would still have three ideas to choose from that my boss felt comfortable with.

Why did we fight so hard for this one particular idea? We had three other perfectly good concepts to go with— and that was the problem.

Good work is on strategy. It's smart, respects the viewer, and is well crafted. You can produce it on time and on budget. Your client can green light it. It makes you comfortable.

Good work is the enemy of great work. If you are satisfied with work that is merely good, you will never deliver great work for your clients.

Great work, like good work, is on strategy. But it's beyond smart; it's something else. Something rare and special. It doesn't just respect the viewer, it connects with the viewer.

Great work might make you uncomfortable. It might be something startlingly new. It might take risks. You might not be able to produce it on time or within budget, and your client might not readily say yes to it.

If the work is truly great, and right for your client, your job is to support it and to help your client see its potential and choose to buy it.

The idea my colleagues and I were fighting for was great, not merely good. It was visually stunning. It spoke the language of the target audience. More than anything else, it was hilariously funny, and humor was the right way to go in this instance.

You might be wondering what happened in the client presentation. The client laughed when we showed the idea to her. She got it, she knew the target would get it. In the end, she didn't love it enough to take a risk on it. The very thing that made the work great—the humor—is the thing that worried her. So she went with a safer choice.

The fault was ours, not hers. We knew the idea was right. We did our best to be persuasive, without applying undue pressure. We wanted her to own the idea with us. We didn't succeed.

We wound up executing a different concept, which made perfectly good advertising. We liked it, and so did the client. But it wasn't great, and we didn't love it.

CHAPTER 14

Don't Fall for Bad Work

What passes for great work these days is often little more than a clever execution or an unusual production technique.

Work like this can be insidious; it masquerades as great advertising, but it is not. Instead it sacrifices the client's advertising objective on an altar of creative self-indulgence. Okay, I admit the metaphor is a little over-wrought, but you get the picture. This kind of advertising is bad, and to see it for what it is requires judgment, dis-passion, and discipline.

It's a much happier task to stand up for work you be-lieve in than it is to speak out against work you know is wrong. But your colleagues will listen to you if you've established yourself as a credible source of input, if you speak with conviction, and if your assessment is well reasoned.

It's not enough to simply say, "I don't know why, but I just don't like it," or "The client won't buy it." You need to explain why the work doesn't deliver on the strategy, why it will fail to engage viewers, why it doesn't deliver the message clearly, or whatever else might be wrong with it.

The easiest way to spot work like this is to ask, "What's the idea driving this advertising?" If there's no idea in what you're seeing, then there isn't anything for the client to buy, and the agency shouldn't be trying to sell it.

CHAPTER 15

Choice Is Good

I've heard of agencies that present just one creative concept to their clients. I've never worked at such an agency, so I can only guess at the motivation behind this approach. Perhaps it's to show confidence that the agency has arrived at *the* solution. Perhaps it's that the agency doesn't have any other ideas.

The agencies I worked at, and most of the other agencies I'm familiar with, have lots of ideas. They know there's more than one way to execute a strategy.

Always bring your client more than one concept. What's the right number? It depends on the client.

Some clients love to see the conference room walls papered with a dozen or more ideas. But that takes time and costs money. It's not always possible, practical, or even desirable. With many clients, showing more than five concepts can be confusing. It also can imply you are surrounding the strategic challenge, rather than solving it.

Generally, the right number of concepts to present is three. It's large enough to provide the client meaningful choice, yet small enough to compel the agency to select only the very best ideas to present.

What do you do if your creative team only comes up with one or two ideas? Do you go to the client with just that one or two? With rare exceptions, I would say no. The best creative people usually have lots of ideas to show you, and if one thing isn't working, they always have something else, or are comfortable going back and concepting some additional ideas. Less talented creative people often have just a single idea to offer, so they will fight fiercely for that idea, regardless of its merit, because they are not confident they can produce more.

It's a matter of knowing your creative team. If you know it will fall short in generating ideas, you need to encourage the creative director to add a second or even a third team to the creative development process. This is not an easy conversation to have, but it's better to deal with this issue at the agency, well before the client presentation, than to go to the client with only the thinnest of presentations. If you do that, you usually wind up going back to the agency anyway to develop more ideas, which costs you time and client goodwill.

Here are three other things to keep in mind when deciding which work to present to the client.

1. Before you present to the client, agree among yourselves what the agency recommendation is among the options, why it is the recommendation, and why the others are not.

2. Decide who will speak for the agency on the recommendation.

3. Make sure you would be proud to execute any of the concepts you show. Eliminate any straw men before the presentation. If it isn't good enough to execute, it isn't good enough to present.

CHAPTER 16

Fight *about* the Work with Colleagues; Fight *for* It with Clients

Years ago, when I was running a major financial services account, I worked with one of my creative director colleagues on a print ad campaign. I'll call him Mel. Mel was a very senior, veteran guy. It was a day or two before we were scheduled to present to the client, and he was walking me through the concepts he was going to show.

Mel was the type of writer who liked to crowd the walls with ideas. It was typical of him to show a dozen or more approaches. For some clients, that many choices would be paralyzing. Not this client. This client loved the theater of it. He loved to debate the ads. He really took ownership of the work, and that was great for us. He welcomed a room full of ideas.

So there I was, looking with Mel at maybe 15 ideas slapped up on the walls of the agency conference room. I liked maybe five of them. Another five or six were serviceable. The rest, I thought, were losers.

Overall I felt great about what I was looking at and said so. I made some suggestions on a couple of the executions. Then I said, "There are a few ads that aren't working." I explained why. In two instances, Mel agreed, and decided to kill the ideas. We disagreed about two or three others. I made my case: The weaker executions would dilute the whole presentation. Besides, we didn't need that many options.

The problem was, Mel thought a couple of the ads I didn't like were among the strongest on the wall. So we went back and forth for a while. Our disagreement never reached the knock-down-drag-out variety, but let's just say it got pretty spirited. Mel put an end to the debate by saying he'd think about it. That's all I could ask for. If I couldn't persuade him, then the trouble was with me, not him.

Two days later we met with the client. Mel took the client through the work. The client liked much of it, but there were two ideas he gravitated to. One was a favorite of mine, the other was one of the ads I wanted to kill, but Mel kept in.

The client turned to me and asked, "So which one would you go with?"

It would have been easy for me to support my choice, trash the one I didn't like. Easy, but wrong.

You owe your colleagues an insightful, expert, candid, and sensitive assessment of their work. (By *work* I don't just mean creative; it could be a strategy recommendation, or a media plan, or something else.) You should base this assessment on your knowledge of the market, your grasp of the consumer's needs and interests, and your understanding of client expectations and culture.

You and your colleagues won't always agree. You will argue; this often is part of arriving at the right solution.

It's fine to fight about the work in private, but once you've agreed on what to present to the client, get on the bus. When you are in front of the client, never throw the work, or your colleagues, under the bus.

I didn't throw the ad I didn't like under the bus. I supported it, and I also supported my choice. But the client wanted a definitive recommendation. Of course, Mel and I were prepared to make one. Prior to the meeting we agreed which one we would go with. So I turned to Mel and said, "Why don't you talk about the choice we arrived at."

Mel did. You probably want to know which one we recommended. The funny thing is, I can't remember. What I do remember is that I fought *about* the work with my colleague, but fought *for* it with my client.

CHAPTER 17

Do Not Sell

W. David Vining, the former director of U.S. advertising and direct marketing at Compaq Computer (now HP) and now a marketing executive at AIMCO, once said, "Too often, a creative-driven agency will try to force their own ideas on a client, rather than working in a spirit of collaboration. It takes a very strong account person to maintain the client's interest, and not take the easy way out by simply selling the work."

David is certainly not alone in this view; I know other clients who share a similar belief.

The problem with selling is that it's about applying pressure on a buyer to do what you want—what is best for you, your colleagues, your agency. Account people often are tempted to be salespeople. By selling the client on the agency's recommendation, you prove your worth to your colleagues. But you do much more damage than good if you take this approach.

You want your client to *buy* great work. Great work almost always entails an element of risk, because there inevitably is something new or unexpected about it. Clients generally will take risks with people they trust. An account person who is busy selling a client is not likely to build trust with that client.

Conversely, an account person who understands that the client's interests are the agency's top priority is going to be viewed as a trusted partner, not as a salesperson for the agency's interests. That kind of account person is in a much better position to credibly recommend that the client take the risk on great work. In the end, that account person is the creative team's greatest ally.

I should be clear about one thing: When I say an account person should make the client's interests the agency's top priority, I am *not* suggesting that the account person is there to simply do the client's bidding or to merely follow the client's commands. Quite the opposite is true. The account person who has established credibility with a client is in the best position to challenge, when necessary, that client's assumptions, demands, and opinions.

Great account people do not sell. Instead, they serve as partners to both their colleagues and to their clients, with a responsibility to facilitate the creation of great work, and a goal of helping clients make the right decisions about that work.

CHAPTER 18

Bring Your Clients
into the Process Early

Advertising isn't just about collaboration within the walls of the agency; it's about collaborating with the client.

No matter how well versed you are in the client's business, your client brings a critical point of view to the process. Most of my clients have forgotten more than I ever knew about their companies and their brands, and that's not because I wasn't immersed in their business. It's just that my clients bring years of experience to the table, experience working inside their companies, experience I could never begin to fully comprehend, let alone duplicate.

I've always understood the benefit of taking advantage of that. At the outset of a new relationship or a new assignment, I tell my clients, "The agency is going to work incredibly hard on this, but we're going to ask you to work hard with us. We need you to be actively involved. We can't do great work for you unless you help us."

Then I ask the clients to outline what they expect from the agency and how they would like to work.

Having this kind of client input helps avoid false starts. Early involvement also gives the client a sense of ownership of the work. This is incredibly important when it comes time for the client to champion the work to the company's employees and management.

So don't hesitate to get your client involved early and often. The work will be better for it, as will the process of creating it.

CHAPTER 19

Respect What It Takes to Do Great Creative

My colleagues and I used to love to present to one particular client.

He was a very senior, very veteran, very smart guy. Whenever we would present, he would listen with great concentration. He would rarely interrupt; instead, he would let us go through all the concepts and options we had prepared for his review.

When we were done, he would stand up to address us. We presented to him many times, but his initial response would always go something like this: "First, I want to thank all of you for your hard work. It's clear from the presentation that you put a tremendous amount of thought and effort into the assignment, and I appreciate that. And there are some terrific ads on the table. Now let's go through each of the concepts one by one so I can give you feedback."

Sometimes the input was minor; most of the time it was significant and as a result we had to reconcept. No one ever complained; creative people loved this client and would do anything for him. We did work for this client that was the best the agency could do.

What was this client's secret? It was simple. No matter what we presented, no matter how great, how good, or how average it was, this client invariably expressed respect for the work and the people who made it. That was a great lesson for me.

In my early days as an account person, I usually ran roughshod over creative people and their work. Writers and art directors would show me concepts and I'd immediately say what was wrong with them. It didn't matter that I might be right; I was serving up the input wrong, and creative people simply tuned me out.

I didn't understand that my job was to *improve* the work, not *approve* it. If I had made that one small adjustment in language and attitude, it would have made a big difference in the way I looked at creative work.

I also didn't respect what it takes to do great creative. What it takes is enormous emotional commitment. When writers or art directors show their work, they are sharing a piece of themselves. They have sweated those ideas to life, and they know they are only as good as their last idea. If you don't respect that—and in the beginning I didn't, but I learned—you have no hope of helping to make the work better.

While it takes emotional commitment to make creative work, it takes emotional detachment to make it better. Creative people don't always have the emotional detachment to evaluate and improve their work. Sometimes they mistake good work for great work. On occasion, they might even mistake bad work for great work.

Who can blame them, given what it takes to produce work in the first place? That's where smart, sensitive account people can, with great judgment and diplomacy, make a big contribution. They can provide the necessary emotional detachment to make the work better, or to prevent bad work from seeing the light of day.

You can't go about this the way I used to, by launching in with a salvo of criticism. There's a better way to provide feedback.

For example, if you're looking at a range of ideas and some are killers, some have potential, and some need to be killed, start with the killer ideas. Acknowledge them, praise them, and explain what you love about them and why.

Then with the ideas that have potential, start with what's right about each of them. Praise what's working. Then talk about what's not working and why. Suggest how these ideas can be made better.

Tackle the ideas that deserve early death last. Even here, with ideas you think are marginal at best, there probably is something you like about each of them. Find that one thing and acknowledge it before explaining why you think the ideas should be abandoned in favor of the stronger ones. If there are lots of good and even great ideas on the table, this should be relatively painless, unless there is sharp disagreement between you and the creative team. If that's the case, keep an open mind as to why the creative people like an idea that you don't. Perhaps you can be persuaded. Perhaps you can persuade them. You're going to need to reach an agreement, because when you visit the client, you want to present a unified front.

Keep your personal preferences out of the discussion. You are not there to render judgment on whether or not periwinkle is the right color. However, if you know the client hates periwinkle, or if periwinkle is the competitor's brand color, by all means speak up.

Here's an example of what I mean. I remember being in a preproduction meeting where we were going over the casting for a photo shoot. We were looking at headshots of kids. Everyone liked this adorable redheaded boy. That's when I spoke up. "The client doesn't like redheaded children; they remind her of clowns and she thinks clowns are scary."

Everybody looked at me as if I were crazy. I explained that this had come up before, on another assignment for this client, when I was working with a different creative team. "You can go in with the redheaded kid," I said, "but I'd have a back-up if I were you. And don't be surprised if the client gets annoyed about your recommendation."

There were lots of cute kids to choose from. We went with another kid. It wasn't worth fighting over hair color.

In reviewing the creative work, your job is to ensure the work is on strategy, to bring a client perspective to the discussion, to measure the work against what is going on in the category, to help determine if the work passes the "So what?" test, and to ensure that no mandatory has been missed (like no redheaded kids).

Above all, your job is to push for great, if what you're seeing is merely good.

CHAPTER 20

Client Presentations Are as Important as New Business Presentations

Agencies treat new business presentations with the intensity and urgency of opening night at the theater.

Everyone knows what's at stake. There is careful consideration given to casting the presenters. There is heavy investment in staging and props. Every word of the script is thought through. The pitch team rehearses. Then it rehearses some more.

But with existing clients, everyone at the agency is so busy making the work that they often neglect the presenting part. With clients demanding faster and faster turn around, and with agency staffs sliced to the bone due to financial pressures, the problem has grown acute. Almost every account person I know can tell stories of flying out the door to make a client meeting while jamming work completed just minutes before into a presentation case. Rehearsal, such as it is, takes place in the 15-minute cab ride to the client's office.

Yet client presentations are at least as important as new business presentations, if not more so. The stakes are just as high, if not higher. The only thing worse than losing a new business pitch is losing a client. If you don't pay attention to client presentations, if you take them for granted, that is the risk.

Client presentations, like new business presentations, are about theater. A bad presentation, like bad theater, often leads to a bad ending, with the client unhappy and the agency scrambling to regroup. A good presentation usually leads to a happy ending, with the client satisfied and the work approved.

A good presentation is no accident. It requires proper casting, with an eye to who can best deliver the material. It requires thoughtful preparation, with particular attention paid to anticipating client concerns and how best to address them. Above all, it requires sufficient time to rehearse, to ensure everyone understands his or her role and how to play it.

Agencies that understand the importance of rehearsing for new business presentations often forget that rehearsing for client presentations is equally important.

Part of the problem is that many agency people hate rehearsing and will do everything to avoid it, no matter how much time there is in the schedule. They find rehearsing awkward, embarrassing, or even a little intimidating. They have a point. It can be harder to stand up in front of colleagues than clients. But doing so can make a huge difference in your team's presentation and professionalism.

Rehearsal helps you discover holes in your argument. It helps you anticipate the questions and concerns the client might raise. It polishes your delivery. It allows you to work out the hand-offs among the team members. It gives everyone in the group an opportunity to help strengthen each member's part. It can build your confidence. For all these reasons, you should remind your colleagues that, no matter how pressed for time all of you are, no matter how tight the schedule, rehearsal might make the difference between success and failure. Then you should take ownership of the rehearsal process.

Set the rehearsal time, drag people into the conference room, get them to agree on their roles, get everyone to agree on the agency recommendation (if what you're presenting is creative work), and then make them stand up and present their parts. The more time you spend, the better you will be. Even if the run-through is lightning fast, it's better than no rehearsal time.

Still, I'm a realist. I know there will be times when rehearsal just won't happen. You and your colleagues will race out of the agency to get to the client on time, then wing it once you're there. That's why the next chapter, No Understudies on Presentation Day, is so important.

CHAPTER 21

No Understudies on Presentation Day

It was an incredibly painful moment. My agency team and I were presenting a new campaign to the client. One of the team members, a young copywriter, was standing at the head of a long conference table, in front of a sea of expectant faces, including our main client's boss, the company's senior vice president of marketing. It was a big day, a big room, and a big group of clients.

The presentation started well enough. I had done the set-up for the writer, taking the audience through a re-statement of the assignment and a quick recap of the creative brief. I turned to the copywriter. He could barely speak. A look of fear came over his face. It quickly became apparent that everything he wanted to say had fled from his head. "Uh, ah, why don't I just go right to the work?" he said, and with that he pulled out the presentation boards.

We had three concepts to show. He raced through each one in about a minute. He couldn't wait to sit down.

It was painful to watch him. I wanted to rescue him, but any intervention on my part would only have added to his humiliation.

The clients were sympathetic; his distress was visible. Their response was muted, their questions restrained. But they didn't buy a single idea we presented. We promised to come back in three days with new work.

After the meeting broke up, my primary client contact asked, "What happened up there?" pointing to the front of the room. "I really don't know," I responded, "I'm sorry; I thought we were prepared. It's clear we weren't." I assured my client that for the next presentation, the creative director would be there and would take the lead. The client's only response was, "I'd better go see my boss; I might as well take my beating now."

We embarrassed ourselves. We embarrassed our client in front of her boss. We undermined our grip on the account. The biggest damage was to the copywriter, who was shaken by his meltdown. "I don't know what happened to me," he said. "I just lost it. It's never happened before."

It wasn't the writer's fault. It was mine. The writer clearly was overmatched by the challenge of making a big presentation to an important client in an intimidating environment. I should have insisted that his boss make the presentation. I had thought this would be a good opportunity for the writer, an occasion he would rise to. I was so wrong. It's a lesson I've never forgotten.

It's important to give junior people a chance to present. How else will they learn? But those learning opportunities need to be confined to *internal* agency presentations—

the young copywriter to the creative director, the young account executive to the group account director—until that star of the future has earned a role in the present, and is proven ready to perform in front of the client.

Until that time, presenting to the client should be left to those most effective at it, and that usually means the more senior people in the shop (any senior person who is a weak presenter needs to address that weakness). There is too much riding on the presentation to do otherwise.

You are not only presenting work, you are representing the agency. Every presentation offers an opportunity to validate the client's confidence in the agency, or conversely, to undermine it.

So there should be no understudies on presentation day. That's when the veterans, the stars, should perform. That's what the client has a right to expect. That is what the client is paying for. That is what will keep the business right where it is, at your agency.

CHAPTER 22

No Scenery Chewers,
No Dead Bodies

Shortly after the head of marketing joined my client, she called a review. My colleagues and I presented to the new marketing chief a couple of weeks later.

I led a five-person pitch team, but you would have thought I was a team of one. I gave most of our presentation and answered most of the client questions. I thought it went pretty well.

Later, after we lost the account, I learned that the client felt we didn't have the depth of senior talent she needed. No wonder; I barely allowed my colleagues to speak. I didn't give them room to demonstrate how smart they were. Instead, I was too busy trying to show how smart I was.

Advertising is about collaboration. So is the presentation of advertising. It is not a one-person show; it's an ensemble performance. There should be no scenery chewers who have all the lines, and who completely dominate the stage.

By the same token, there should be no dead bodies. Everyone present from the agency should have a role. If a person doesn't have a role, he or she shouldn't be in the room. You don't want the clients asking themselves, "Why is that person here? What value is that person adding? Why am I paying for that person?"

CHAPTER 23

Be Prepared to Throw Away the Script

We were supposed to have an hour to present. My colleagues and I figured we could calibrate our presentation for 45 minutes, to leave time for questions and discussion. When the clients were late, we assumed they would extend our time to compensate. They didn't. Instead, they said, "You've got 20 minutes."

We thought we were well prepared, but we hadn't prepared for that. Caught off-guard, we didn't know how to edit ourselves on the fly, and as a result, came off poorly.

Just because you've prepared to present a certain way doesn't mean you'll get to do it exactly the way you intended. Clients have their own agendas, and you have to be ready to bend yours to theirs.

After you lay out your roadmap for the presentation, but before you launch in, ask the client, "Are you comfortable with the plan? Anything we've missed?" If the client wants the presentation to go in a different order, or even a different direction, from what you planned, you should be ready to adjust.

What's the point of insisting on your agenda, only to have your words land on a tuned-out audience? If you've rehearsed, if you've anticipated what the client might ask, you'll be in a good position to be flexible, fast on your feet, and ready to ad-lib.

CHAPTER 24

The More Informal You Want to Be, the More Rehearsed You Need to Be

If you're presenting with PowerPoint (or some other presentation software), if you're relying on charts or boards, if you're reading from notes, presenting is relatively easy. You have a safety net.

However, if you're *talking* with your audience, rather than *presenting* to it—without computer slides, without boards or notes—you are working without a net. It's harder and riskier, but it's often more effective. In some cases, it's necessary.

For example, if you are doing a set-up to a creative presentation, PowerPoint slides don't work, and relying on notes is less than ideal. A creative set-up usually takes only a few minutes, but those few minutes of conversation set the tone for what's to follow. Of course, *what* you choose to say is most important, but *how* you say it is a close second. The ability to talk the set-up with a combination of confidence and informality tends to work best.

If you're going to present without slides, boards, or notes, you need to really rehearse so that you are confident enough to appear relaxed and informal. It is a rare person who can wing it and do well. Most seemingly casual presenters invest in practice time. So if you want or need to work without a net, make sure you take time to prepare.

CHAPTER 25

Know Your Opening Cold

Early in my career I flew with my boss, the agency CEO, and two other colleagues to Detroit to make a major presentation to some marketing people at one of the big three auto companies. I had a major role in the presentation, and to say I was nervous would understate my knee-knocking anxiety.

We arrived a half hour early and were shown into a conference room. As we were setting up for the presentation, my boss erupted. "What's this?" He pointed to one of my slides. I don't remember what the problem was, but I clearly remember the look on his face. He was one unhappy guy.

If this happened today, I could have simply changed the offending slide on my computer, but this happened back in the pre–notebook computer age, when overhead projectors ruled the earth. There was no way to change the overhead transparency. My boss was really upset, and he was upsetting me.

"Look," I said, "we've got to present in a couple of minutes, and this isn't helping. There's nothing I can do about the problem. We're both going to have to live with it." With that, I excused myself and went to look for the men's room.

I tried to compose myself. If I was nervous before, now I was downright panicky. But I didn't give in to it. Instead, I got mad, and vowed that I wasn't going to let my boss's comments throw me off my game.

In the men's room, I went over my opening again. I had really rehearsed for this presentation, and I had paid particular attention to my opening remarks. It was still all there, lodged safely in my brain. I took a deep breath, and went back to the conference room to meet the clients. When it was my turn to present, I got up and delivered my slides with confidence. The problem my boss was so freaked out about didn't even surface as an issue.

I got through my presentation mainly because I knew my opening cold.

If you're going to falter, it is likely to happen in your opening, and a screw-up in the opening is likely to compound itself. You feel bad about the mistake, it throws you off, and you make another mistake. Before you know it, you're tripping all over yourself.

That's why you need to know your opening the way you know the first words of the Gettysburg Address. After you nail your opening, you'll relax. When you relax, the rest of your presentation will flow. You will enjoy yourself. It will show, and the presentation will be a success.

CHAPTER 26

Better to Have It and Not Need It, Than to Need It and Not Have It

Are you familiar with the "umbrella theory" of life? The theory goes like this: If it looks like rain, carry an umbrella and there won't be any. The theory applies not just to rain, but to account management. The idea is to anticipate what might happen and prepare for it. Chances are it won't happen, but if it does, you'll be ready. It's the way to stay out of the rain in dealing with clients.

I remember once being in a second round creative presentation when the client asked, "Can I take another look at the idea I killed the last time we met?" I looked at the creative director; she looked at me. We both had assumed the work was dead, and didn't think to bring it with us. I never let that happen again. I don't care if I'm on the fifth round of creative presentations; I make sure I have all the work from the previous rounds.

For a different creative presentation, I remember rushing to get all the work together, and neglecting to bring a copy of the creative brief. I didn't realize my oversight until we were in the meeting and I went fumbling in my briefcase for the brief that wasn't there. I sure didn't look like the buttoned-up account executive I thought myself to be. Instead, I looked pretty foolish.

In the barely controlled chaos that often precedes a client presentation, it's easy to forget something, or to find yourself scrambling to locate a document that suddenly becomes the focus of the discussion. So I suggest you make a checklist for yourself. This will force you to anticipate the questions or issues that might arise in the discussion, then will help you create and compile all the materials you might need to respond.

As you try to squeeze a two-foot pile of stuff into your ultra-thin, ultra-cool briefcase, remember that it's better to have it and not need it than to need it and not have it. Even if you have to walk into the meeting with a shopping bag bursting with background material.

CHAPTER 27

Support What You Say

I remember an instance when a single unsupported assertion derailed an entire presentation.

My agency colleagues and I were presenting an ad campaign to a prospective client. Key to the campaign was a particular celebrity spokesperson. We believed this spokesperson was perfect for the client, and for the audience we were trying to reach.

We just assumed the client would agree with us. So when the client asked us for some data or research to support our recommendation, all we could do is offer more opinions. We found ourselves saying "We think this" and "We feel that" when what the client wanted to hear is "Here's what we *know*, and here are the facts to back it up." Our lack of supporting data made us look unprofessional.

We *probably* were right about the celebrity working well for this client, but the client was *unequivocally* right to expect us to make a sound case for our recommendation. When we didn't, we undermined our credibility and sabotaged our entire presentation. Needless to say, we didn't get the account.

Well before you make a presentation, check it for any claims it makes. If there's an opinion that won't stand up to a client's challenge, make sure you go back and build a case for it. If you find you can't build a case for that opinion, you're better off keeping it to yourself.

CHAPTER 28

Listening Is More Important Than Talking

At a major presentation for a big piece of business, my colleagues and I came prepared with what we thought was powerful strategic insight and dazzling creative. We presented with great self-assurance for more than 90 minutes. When we were done, we asked, "Are there any questions?"

The room was silent. Then the lead client stood up and said, "Very impressive. It's clear you thought long and hard about our business. Speaking on behalf of my colleagues, I want to thank you for all your effort. You'll be hearing from us in about a week."

We were dumbstruck. No questions? Not a single one? All we could do was thank the clients for their time, shake their hands, and leave.

A week later we heard from the client. The company had selected another agency.

It should have come as no surprise to us. During our presentation, we did all the talking. Not one of us thought to stop and ask the clients, "How do you feel about this?" or, "That's our opinion; what's yours?" or, "Am I being clear on this point?"

We came off as arrogant and tone deaf. I later learned the client felt browbeaten and excluded.

We should have known then what I know now: If, at the end of your presentation, you and your colleagues have done all the talking, you will know that you have failed.

The goal isn't to deliver your lines exactly as rehearsed. The goal isn't to make all of the points you want to make. The goal is to be effective, and that means engaging the client, as early and as often as possible, in a discussion that leads to a sharing of ideas and opinions, and that ultimately leads to a meeting of the minds.

In one of the best new business pitches I ever participated in, my colleagues and I never actually got to present. We certainly were prepared, but the client preferred to talk, and we let him. It led to a freewheeling, wide-ranging discussion. We went well over our allotted time. Ultimately we were awarded the account.

It was the best presentation I *never* made.

Running a meeting . . .

CHAPTER 29

Start on Time, End on Time

Does anyone in advertising pay attention to this simple rule? I doubt it. Okay, with client meetings agencies certainly try to be punctual. But then the clients usually keep the agency waiting. If the problem is chronic with your clients, you have two options: 1) put up with it, or 2) gently, very gently, remind them they are paying for all those people cooling their heels in the conference room.

With internal meetings at the agency, usually everyone keeps everyone else waiting. You can do something about it, however. If it's your meeting, start it on time. If it's someone else's meeting, show up on time. If the meeting leader isn't there, or isn't ready to start, give him or her ten minutes, then leave. Do that a couple of times and people will get the message.

With everyone on call to clients, there are going to be occasions when people will be late for internal meetings. The goal is to make that the exception, not the rule. The idea is to respect your colleagues' time, which allows you to ask for the same in return.

Once a meeting is underway, the goal should be to make it as short as possible. Get it done so everyone can get out and do the work.

Another secret to meetings that respect everyone's time is to have fewer of them. If people are chronically late to meetings, it might be the result of too many meetings that add too little value to the work process. So when you call a meeting, be certain it's necessary, invite only the people who need to be there, and make sure you accomplish what you set out to accomplish. If you do these things, you will become known as a person who gets things done. People might be late to other meetings, but they'll show up on time for yours.

CHAPTER **30**

Have an Agenda
and Stick to It
(Most of the Time)

The process of creating an agenda in advance helps you determine if you actually *need* a meeting, or if a phone call or an e-mail will do. I'm a big believer in face-to-face contact, but I also know that too many meetings can impede work rather than advance it. That's the test: Ask yourself if the meeting will advance the work. If the answer is no, or if the answer is that I can accomplish the same objective as effectively without a meeting, then don't have it.

Assuming the meeting is necessary, you should create an agenda, and not just in your head. Putting it on paper shows respect for the other participants. It also gives you a way to solicit input. This is particularly important when preparing for client meetings. You want your client's input before you get in the conference room. Nothing undermines efficiency worse than convening a group, only to find there is disagreement over the meeting's purpose and content.

At the meeting itself, the agenda provides focus, and helps keep you on course. Start by asking if everyone is comfortable with what's planned. If it's a client meeting, be particularly sensitive to the client's wishes. Restate the meeting duration: "This should take us about 30 minutes."

The agenda should be your guide, but don't let it control you—you should control it. Agendas are not written in stone, and agencies are in the idea business. If a meeting takes an unexpected but promising turn, be prepared to go with the flow. I've been in meetings where, quite unexpectedly, wonderful discoveries were made or insights revealed. In some of these situations, my agency colleagues and I were meeting on something quite unrelated to the breakthrough we achieved. That's a great meeting.

CHAPTER 31

Be Brief, Be Bright,
Be Gone

I've been trapped in a thousand meetings and conversations that have gone twice as long as they needed to. I'm sure I've been as long-winded as the next person.

The way to shorten those meetings and conversations is to come to the table prepared. Know what you want the outcome of the meeting, the conversation, or the presentation to be. Say what you have to say quickly, clearly, and concisely. Don't waste your clients' or colleagues' time. The workday is long enough as it is.

Above all, know when to close your briefcase. Once you have buy-in, it's time to move on. If you continue to talk, you might talk people out of what they just agreed to.

I know one CEO who can be very persuasive. He has just one flaw: He doesn't know when to shut up. He makes his case—people often agree with him—but then he keeps talking, and before long those he persuaded are rethinking their decision.

You're probably wondering who that CEO is. It's me.

CHAPTER 32

Lead the Meeting, Don't Tyrannize It

Your role is to guide the discussion, to keep everyone on track, and to ensure you efficiently accomplish what needs to get done, while leaving room for productive detours and digressions. You want to make sure all voices are heard, and actively seek participation from those who are more inclined to listen than contribute.

If anything is unclear, your job is to make sure it becomes clear by probing the other people in the room or on the phone. It's important to grasp not only the text of what people are saying, but also the unspoken subtext.

With clients, there will be times when you detect a subtext to a comment or a reaction, but choose to deal with it privately, after the meeting. You'll have to judge when this is the best course of action.

For example, if the subject of cost comes up in a large group meeting, it sometimes is better to take the conversation offline, where you and your client can speak privately.

Let's say you're in a large group meeting and you observe the client being short with one person on your agency team. It could be nothing, or it could be a sign of a bigger, deeper problem. You don't want to ignore the sign, but you certainly don't want to pursue it in a roomful of people. The right course of action is to follow-up in private with your client.

In-person meetings are easy to run compared with teleconferences, but teleconferences are an unfortunate reality, especially with out-of-town colleagues or clients.

On the speakerphone you don't have the advantage of face-to-face contact, or the clues of body language. Voice inflections become muddy. So you need to work extra hard to ensure all views are expressed and heard. You must pay extra attention to hear the subtext of any client commentary.

Every meeting should have a well-defined ending, where you recap any decisions reached, next steps to be taken, and who owns them. This requires not only that you listen well, but also that you take careful notes.

In short, meetings matter. It's your responsibility to facilitate the desired outcome by leading, not dominating, the discussion.

CHAPTER 33

Always Follow Up

This has happened to me more times than I care to remember: I meet with a client to go over a creative brief or something similar. We discuss, negotiate, agree. Or so I think. The next time we meet, I hear "That's not what we agreed to."

Sometimes I'm dealing with a client who suffers from a convenient form of memory loss, which seems to only affect his or her ability to recall our last discussion. Colleagues are not immune from the disease either, and I admit I myself have suffered from it on occasion. Other times it's not a case of selective memory; instead something really did get lost in translation. You finish a discussion, you think you have consensus, only to discover there is a disconnect somewhere.

That's why it's critical to follow up every meeting, every call, every decision. Never assume there is closure; secure closure. Immediately after the meeting concludes, follow up with an e-mail conference report.

It is not necessary to revisit the discussion. Simply bullet the decisions reached and the next steps required.

You should do this for all meetings, but it is crucial for client meetings, because it provides an audit trail. Should a dispute arise later in the process, the conference reports will quickly confirm who agreed to what, and when.

Have I been clear? Or do I need to go over this again?

PART TWO

Relationships

"No, Thursday's out. How about never—is never good for you?"

Attitude

CHAPTER 34

Judgment Overrides Any Rule

Martin Puris, cofounder and former CEO of the great agency Ammirati & Puris, has said, "The job of account executive is the most difficult in the agency business. It's an intellectual high-wire act.

"The two fatal mistakes an account person can make are to become either the client's 'man' at the agency—or the agency's 'man' at the client.

"Both fail.

"A good account person gives us objectivity, commitment, insight and—above all—truth."

It is no small challenge to counterbalance client demands with agency realities, and to manage money and time when both have become increasingly scarce. The deeper challenge is to have the judgment needed to do and say exactly the right thing in exactly the right way to exactly the right person at exactly the right time.

Some account people seem to have great instincts about this. But I'll bet if you look deeper you'll find that there's more to their judgment skills than just good instincts. I'll bet you'll find that the account people with the best judgment are the ones who made mistakes and learned from them. Their *good* judgment comes in part from previous *bad* judgment.

This is a book of rules, but an account executive works in a world of exceptions. No rule can accommodate every situation, and no list of rules is exhaustive. In the end, the only rule you can rely on is this: Judgment rules.

CHAPTER **35**

Credit Is for
Creative Directors

Did you see the film *Wag the Dog*? The character played by Dustin Hoffman is called Stanley Motss. Stanley is a movie producer. At one point in the movie he does a riff on how everyone knows what the directors and actors do, but no one understands what a producer does. Later, he insists, "I want the credit!" Instead of getting the credit, he gets murdered. A lesson to us all.

Poor Stanley might just as well have been an agency account executive. If you're worried about getting the credit, I suggest you think about another line of work. As an account exec, your job is to give the credit—to your clients, to your colleagues—not to take it. Often, the only people who truly appreciate what you do are other account people.

Years ago, a creative team I was working with wanted to present some envelope-pushing work to our client. I knew my client tended to quickly kill new thinking if it made her even slightly nervous. So I called the client the day before the presentation and said, "Do you have time for dinner this evening?" She did.

We went without anyone else from the agency or her company. We had a great time talking about everything except work. When the time was right, I said, "Look, you're going to see some great concepts tomorrow. The creative team worked incredibly hard on the assignment, and they're really excited about what they have to show you. All of the work is really smart, but some of the best stuff is pretty edgy. Try to keep an open mind. If something concerns you, let's not kill it out-of-hand. Let's talk about it first." She agreed.

The next day, the presentation went really well, and the client bought the agency's recommendation. On the way back to the agency, the creative director said, "That was a surprise. I was expecting a fight. I wasn't expecting the client to approve our recommendation."

To which I answered, "The work was great, and you did an amazing job presenting it." Then I smiled. I knew I had helped achieve the right outcome, and that was good enough for me. The creative team could have the credit. They earned it.

CHAPTER 36

You Cannot Lead
an Account from Your Desk

When I worked at a Boston-based agency, my main client was in New York. That company worked with multiple agencies; our shop was the only one not in New York. I learned early on that if we were going to hold our own against the competitors, I would have to spend more time in New York than Boston. I earned an astonishing number of frequent flyer miles shuttling between the two cities.

If I didn't have any New York client meetings scheduled for a particular week, I would pick a day and plan a visit there anyway. I'd call a couple of my client contacts and say, "Hey, I have to be in New York on Thursday. You around that day? I'd love to stop in to say hello." That's how I would fill my calendar. In between the meetings I scheduled I would walk the halls to say hello to my other contacts. Many times I'd get pulled into an office for an impromptu conversation.

It was a great way to serve my clients. I knew it was working when one of my client contacts awarded my shop a new assignment and said, "You guys are in Boston, but I see you here way more than the New York agencies."

Account work is fieldwork. You need to visit your clients regularly, no matter if they are on the next street or in the next time zone. Phone calls and e-mails don't replace face time.

Don't wait for trouble before you get off your butt. Spend time with clients when things are going well. Most clients have little patience for account people who only show up when something goes wrong. If that's the only time you see your client, then you won't have forged the relationship you need in order to fix the problem you're there to address.

I once worked with an agency executive who didn't like to travel to the city where one of our largest clients was located. My colleague was a very senior guy, critical to building a relationship with top management. During the years the agency worked with this client, my colleague was an all-too-infrequent presence at client headquarters.

The client fired us after some ongoing issues that we couldn't seem to get resolved. There were lots of reasons why we were dismissed. One of them, I think, was a lack of attention from our agency's senior management. The client's CEO found it too easy to fire us; there was no relationship at the top. Perhaps if there had been one, the outcome would have been different.

It is almost impossible to spend too much time with clients. So, if you lack a specific reason to see your clients, create one.

CHAPTER 37

Avoid the Dark Side

You've probably read about top account people who develop such a close personal relationship with their clients that they are said to "own" the account. In truly extreme cases, an account person can shop the client to competing agencies. If the account person switches agencies, the client switches with them.

I can't begin to say how completely, utterly unethical this is. Yes, one of your primary responsibilities is to forge a strong bond with your client. Yes, people work with people, not with organizations. But this does not give you license to ignore your obligations to the agency that employs you. This is the primary reason agencies now make senior executives sign nonsolicit, noncompete agreements that are designed to prevent account people from taking clients with them when they switch agencies.

Your job is to build a strong client relationship on behalf of your agency, *not* on behalf of yourself. You do not own the client relationship; you are merely the keeper of it. You have a fiduciary and an ethical responsibility to do everything in your power to ensure that the client feels loyal not just to you, but to other people in the agency, and to the agency as a whole.

If you have done your best to facilitate ties between your client and the agency, the client is much less likely to go with you if you change agencies. If the client does decide to find a new agency after you've left, you'll know that it wasn't due to any shortcoming on your part, but rather on a shortcoming at the shop you left behind. You'll be known as a person of integrity. In the context of a long career, that is far more valuable than any short-term gain you might derive from an account you are able to transport to a new agency.

CHAPTER 38

Great Work Wins Business; a Great Relationship Keeps It

In new business pitches, clients often claim to seek a relationship with the agency, yet select the winner based on which shop presented the work they liked best. Conversely, with existing accounts, clients often say it's the work that matters, yet fire the agency because of a breakdown in the relationship.

Think of all the client-agency marriages that dissolved, even though they were characterized by great work. BMW and Ammirati & Puris. Ikea and Deutsch. Taco Bell and TBWA\Chiat\Day. Charles Schwab and BBDO. Staples and Cliff Freeman. Add your own examples. The list can get very, very long.

I remember what one client said to me years ago, "I love your work; the agency is very creative. But you guys are just too hard to deal with; everything is a fight. If I have to choose, I'll take an agency a little less talented but a whole lot easier to work with."

And then she fired us.

We had won the account based on our work. We lost the account because we didn't understand that while great work is what wins business, a great relationship is what keeps it. We thought if we did great work, the relationship stuff would take care of itself. Advertising isn't just a creative business, though; it's a relationship business.

I don't mean relationship as in "doing lunch," although there certainly is a time and place for that. I mean relationship as in doing all of the things, and being all of the things, that build trust with the client. Listening. Asking the right questions. Anticipating and solving problems. Meeting commitments. Managing expectations. Eliminating unpleasant surprises. Taking ownership. Acting with integrity.

A client who trusts you will seek your counsel. A client who trusts you will forgive your honest mistakes, and will work with you to correct them. A client who trusts you will partner with you in taking the risks that lead to great work.

A relationship is like a brand: you have to invest in it, and understand that it gets built over time. You can't rush it; even the slightest hint of insincerity, dishonesty, or manipulation will kill a relationship before it has a chance to develop.

Whenever I hear someone say, "The work is the only thing that matters," I think of the client who fired me years ago. It reminds me that if you don't pay attention to building a strong relationship with your client, you run the risk of being shown the door, no matter how terrific the work.

Advertising *is* about the work, but remember that advertising is a business. Business is about relationships, and a great relationship allows great work to flourish.

CHAPTER 39

We Are Smarter Together Than We Are Alone

At the signing of the Declaration of Independence, Ben Franklin said to his Continental Congress colleagues, "We must all hang together, or assuredly we shall all hang separately." Ben of course was worried about the British. The reason I pay attention to Ben is I worry about the enemies of great advertising.

The creation of advertising and everything that surrounds it—the plans, presentations, budgets, and schedules—is a collaborative process. Effective collaboration is key to making great advertising. So why are so many agencies siloed? Why do departments within agencies—account management, creative, media—often act more like competitors than colleagues? Why is it that many agencies are characterized by turf battles, warring egos, and petty politics?

I suppose you could excuse some of this because of the inherently nonlinear, dysfunctional nature of creating advertising. But much of it, I think, is the result of people forgetting who and what the enemies are.

To get your colleagues to hang together, remind them that the enemy is the competition. The enemy is never having enough time to do the work. The enemy is whatever stands in the way of making great work.

Remind your colleagues that you need one another in order to create the best possible advertising in the most efficient and cost-effective way. Remind them you are smarter together than you are alone.

Above all, remind them that if you don't hang together and help one another, you *will* hang separately, soon after the client replaces your agency with another.

Communication

CHAPTER 40

Make No Commitment
without Consultation

As a young account executive starting out in the business, I had the good fortune to work with the client from hell. I don't know if this client hated agencies in general, or simply hated me in particular, but it seemed as if I could do no right.

I dreaded telephone calls from this client; I would flinch before picking up the phone. Meetings were worse; I'd lie awake the night before in dread.

I remember one particularly difficult discussion about a schedule. The client was biting: "It takes you guys longer to write an ad than it took Tolstoy to write *War and Peace*. I want to see copy two days from now, not two weeks from now. Okay?"

I didn't know it at the time, but this was a test. I was intimidated by this client. When he said "Okay?" it was strictly rhetorical. He meant, "Get it done, you worthless bag carrier!"

The easy way out would have been to say, "You got it!" and beat a hasty retreat, but I knew that would only delay worse pain. There was no way we could have copy to him in two days, and when we failed to deliver, all the client's rage would be visited on me.

I also knew that saying no would mean rage right there. He'd pick up the phone, call my boss, and scream at her.

So, in an instant, I said, "Let me make a quick call and see what we can do." The client looked at me derisively. "Sure, go ahead and call your pals." I stepped out of his office, found a phone, and spoke with my creative colleagues. After I did some begging and pleading, they agreed to have something to the client in four days.

I went back to the client and said, "I know you want it in two days, but how about four days? That's a big improvement over two weeks."

His answer: "Three days." To which I replied, "John, I can push the creatives to three days, but it isn't enough time to get the work right. We'll wind up having to do a major rewrite and take even more time. Give us the four days and we'll nail it."

"It better be brilliant," was his reply.

When I got back to the agency, the creatives weren't happy, but they knew what I was dealing with in this client, and they understood. They delivered in four days.

I didn't have an entirely happy client. I didn't have an entirely happy group of colleagues. But I had managed to broker a solution without the client asking my boss to fire me, and without my colleagues thinking I had sold them down the river.

What I took away from this experience is to make no commitment without consultation.

When a client makes a request, let alone a demand, your first, and understandable, instinct is to say yes. The more senior the client, the more urgent the need, the more strident the tone, the more you want to comply on the spot. Don't do it.

Even with seemingly simple requests, a unilateral yes is *not* the right answer. It does a terrible disservice to everyone—your colleagues, yourself, and most of all, your client.

A commitment without consultation ignores the collaborative nature of making advertising. It pays no respect to the people you work with. Besides, you might not be able to deliver on your commitment.

You may be a big fish in the agency food chain. You may have the power to say yes, but you and your client will soon feel the consequences of the unchecked exercise of that power. It will undermine teamwork, erode morale, and destroy your credibility.

The fact is, the more senior you are, the easier it is to explain to your client that you want to check with others before saying yes.

That doesn't mean you say no either. (See Chapter 41.)

The exact answer you give will of course depend on the circumstances, but it should go something like this: "I *think* it will be fine, but give me a minute to check, then get back to you."

Go to your colleagues, gain consensus, then get back to your client, without delay. The client needs an answer, quickly, that all of you can live with.

There Is No *No* in Your Client Vocabulary

Your job is to build bridges, not barriers. *No* is a barrier builder.

So, even when a client makes a seemingly unreasonable request—about a deadline, a budget, a change in the work—*no* is not the answer. *No* helps no one—not the agency, not your colleagues, and of course, not the client.

What is the right answer?

First remember to make no commitment without consultation. Even after you've spoken with your colleagues, you may still not be able to give your clients exactly what they want.

When an unqualified yes isn't possible, offer a qualified one: "Here's what we can do; it's not a perfect solution, but does it address your need?"

Discuss, negotiate, collaborate, solve the problem together. Even difficult clients will usually accept a reasonable solution, especially when you've made every effort to give them what they want.

That's what happened with the story I told about the "client from hell" in Chapter 40. I admit it wasn't much of a negotiation, but I did get the client to accept (grudgingly) a solution a little short of his demand, without completely upsetting my colleagues. I also lived to work another day.

CHAPTER 42

Before You Tell Clients or Colleagues What You *Think,* Tell Them What You *Know*

Everyone has an opinion. And you want to hear their opinions, especially your client's.

You'll be tempted to add yours to the mix. You should. Before you do, remember that your job is to be an expert source on the business—a source not just of opinions, but of facts.

So get the facts on the table first. What you know about the competitors, the customers, or anything else that has a bearing on the discussion. Everyone else has opinions, but as the facts you present demonstrate, yours is an informed one.

CHAPTER 43

Before You Give Clients What They *Need*, First Give Them What They *Want*

I'll often say to clients, "Give us the problem, not the solution. Ask the question; don't give us the answer. Let us solve the problem. That's what you hired us for. We want to help you get to the right place."

Some clients agree, some don't. These days, lots of clients hire agencies to execute, not to think. Clients are not entirely to blame; agencies have contributed to the erosion of their authority with clients. Agencies have been better at making television ads than at solving marketing problems. This has allowed consulting firms to replace ad agencies as chief strategy advisors to "C-level" client executives.

The result is many clients no longer say, "This is the problem I need you to address." Instead, they say, "Here's how I want my problem solved; now go execute some advertising."

If this is what you're confronted with, what do you do?

First, let me advise you on what *not* to do: Do not give in to the temptation to save clients from themselves. If they make a decision, if they give you direction, respect what they say. Be prepared to give them what they've asked for.

However, if what they've asked for is wrong, or if it falls short in any way, you have an obligation to go above and beyond what's called for.

After you've done everything possible to execute the client's direction effectively, you should present other possibilities. Make sure you give the client what they wanted first, then show the client what you think they need.

Presented with a choice, many clients will make a wise decision. Especially if you truly respected their wishes and did the best possible job with the direction they gave you. And especially if you've developed a relationship built on mutual respect and trust.

Still, even the smartest clients will occasionally make choices that are not the smartest. If there is no way to persuade them otherwise, and if there is no way to get them to research or test your recommendation, you'll have to rely on the marketplace to do your persuading for you. Perhaps the next time the client will be more willing to ask the question, rather than provide the answer, and to rely on you and your agency for the solution.

How to Write
a Letter of Proposal

"I like it. It's dumb without trying to be clever."

Writers get to fill their books with broadcast and print ads, some outdoor and Web stuff, and maybe a collateral piece or two. Account people don't have books to showcase their work, but if they did, they would fill them with Word documents and PowerPoint presentations. Not exactly the most scintillating material, it's a better cure for insomnia than anything else. But the reality is, if you want to be a really good account person, you need to master writing a good letter of proposal.

There are some terrific books on how to write well, and I include three in Chapter 57, "Invest Some Time (Again) in These Books." But I also think it would be helpful to explain five things that I think are critical in putting together an effective letter of proposal:

1. *It's an* agreement, *not a* contract. I may be parsing words, but if you allow the lawyers—yours and the client's—to get involved in drafting a contract, the assignment will be over before you sign anything, and the only one to profit will be your attorney.

   In all the years I've been in advertising, I have never needed help arriving at a client agreement. Instead, I've relied on a simple and thorough letter to establish an assignment's scope of work. Once I've completed the letter, I ask my client to sign it before beginning the assignment.

   Letters of proposal do in fact operate as "legal agreements," but by keeping the writing personal and informal, I get to an outcome that's faster, cheaper, and better. And if you deliver on the scope of work you described, you won't need to call your attorney.

2. *Write the way you speak.* You are not trying to replicate "party of the first part" legal language. Write conversationally.

3. *Tell them what you are going to tell them.* After the usual pleasantries that you use to open the letter—"It was great to see you the other day, blah, blah, blah."—make sure you outline what the rest of the letter will entail. The letter should include the following elements:

   - A recap of the assignment

   - A discussion of the various components you plan to include in the scope of work

   - A budget estimate, both for your fees and any third-party costs you might incur (media, production, travel, etc.)

   - A schedule

   - Next steps

   - Another "thanks for the opportunity" closing, with a reminder that you will call to follow up.

4. *Use short paragraphs.* Use headlines to separate the letter into digestible segments. Keep your paragraphs short; six lines maximum is the rule.

5. *Write it, then rewrite it.* The key to getting a letter of proposal that is clear and convincing lies not in the writing but in the rewriting. The editing process will not only sharpen your language, it also will clarify your thinking.

There are countless ways to write a letter of proposal, and I'm certain my approach is just one among many. Still, I thought it would be helpful if I included an example.

The letter that follows is one I sent to a potential client, sanitized to maintain confidentiality and to remove the actual numbers I quoted. Admittedly, it lost a bit of steam as I did my housekeeping, but it still gives you a sense of the approach. (In case you're wondering, I did not get this assignment.)

With apologies to all the really good writers out there, here it is:

SOLOMON STRATEGIC

January 7, 2008

Ms. Jane Doe
CEO
Jane Doe & Company
123 45th Avenue
New Town, California 98765

Re: Website.com proposal

Dear Jane,

I hope you are having a good trip out West. I enjoyed our breakfast meeting and found our conversation about conducting a measurable television advertising test for Website.com to be invigorating.

We spoke by phone shortly thereafter to consider how we might structure a test around the two :30 spots you emailed with just $00,000 to spend. What follows is a proposal that recaps the assignment; discusses creative, production, media, and measurement; and outlines cost and timing.

Assignment Recap

In addition to having a simple, unique, and memorable URL, the Website.com website provides a real service to consumers by making it fast, easy, and convenient to compare various offers, then apply online for the offer that is best suited to their individual needs.

Even in the absence of broad awareness-building advertising, traffic on the site is brisk and growing. But a question remains: can Website.com substantially grow the number of online applications through an advertising effort?

The purpose of the test is to answer this question and to do so for $00,000.

If our goal is merely to drive increased click-throughs to the Website.com website, our test would be relatively simple to construct: choose a test market, pick some dayparts and stations, run the spots as constructed, then measure results.

But our goal is *not* to measure traffic; it is instead to measure *completed orders.*

This makes the assignment more complex, and as a result, there are four issues we need to address: creative execution, production, media, and measurement.

Creative

For starters, the :30 spots don't explain why or how viewers should apply or benefits for doing so. Music choice is admittedly subjective, but there are alternatives to explore that could be more engaging and enticing. You also explained that we don't have permission from the companies to run their brands on television.

In an ideal world, we would create a new direct-response-oriented television (DRTV) spot, geared to encouraging viewers not only to visit Website.com but also to apply for one or more cards when they are on the site. To give us the time we need to tell viewers exactly what we want them to do, and to help us qualify for lower-cost DRTV media, we would create a :60 spot, not a :30.

But the reality is, you've already invested in creating two commercials, and it will be far less expensive for us to convert one of the current :30s into a :60, rather than starting over.

I've watched the spots; I'm confident we can convert either of them into a :60.

We would do this by combining a new voice-over commentary with a range of graphic "slates" that would be intercut into the existing spot. We might, for example, open and close with slates and the new voice-over. We also might insert one or two "breaks" within the commercial itself, to reinforce the message we are trying to convey.

Traditional DRTV marketers would add an incentive to induce the behavior they're seeking, but this isn't something you would consider. Regardless, the goal is to stretch the current :30 into a full :60, without adding any on-air talent and without reshooting any live action.

In the end, we will try to construct a spot that maintains rhythm and flow by designing the breaks to be smooth and efficient. The objective is to create finished advertising that is built as if it was an original :60 DRTV spot.

There's a good bit of creative development to address here. To assist me, I will select a copy/art creative team from among my roster of options. I have several people in mind; my goal will be to select people who can work fast and cheap.

Production

We also need to produce a new spot. We will select an actor for the voice-over and choose a recording studio to lay down the track. We need a company to create the slates we will use. We need to relook at the music, make some recommendations, and arrive at a selection. And we need to edit and mix everything together at a studio, do final conforming, then traffic the spots to the stations on which the ads will run.

All of this is fairly technical work, and to assist me I will hire a freelance producer. I have one in mind whom I've worked with in the past. If he's available and the price is right, it will help. If he isn't, I will need to explore other options.

Media Planning and Buying

With DRTV, the best, most efficient way to buy media is nationally, which allows us to gain the efficiencies of a countrywide cable buy. But with just $00,000 to invest, we need to control cost, which means we will conduct the test in a single market.

I'm not a media expert, and normally I would turn to one of the media planning and buying shops for assistance. I know a number of smaller shops and consultancies who might be willing to take this on at low cost and will explore these.

I also will talk with Comcast, Time Warner, and Cablevision about bypassing the media planning/buying agencies and working with them directly on market and daypart selection. I have contacts at Comcast and Cablevision (both clients) who can help me, and I have a source who can help me with Time Warner.

Regardless of the approach I pursue, I'm assuming we will choose a single market in which we will pick three to five local cable channels to run on and in which we will choose several dayparts. From this, I will construct a very simple media plan for a three- to four-week test.

Measurement

In our initial discussions, we agreed that measurement presents a challenge, given the site doesn't presently embed a means of doing this. But in a subsequent voice mail, you indicated there is a way to capture results.

This clearly requires more discussion, but regardless of the approach, once we select our test market, you will need to create some pre- and post-baseline data on application volume, which can serve as our "control." You then can measure results during and immediately after the spots run in-market. You also should measure results in the weeks that follow to see if applications return to their normal levels.

What we hope to see is a significant increase in volume, at a cost-per that meets or exceeds the target number we establish for the test. We then want to convert this into a story to tell investors, with a projection of what the numbers would be like in a broader rollout. We will need good data, and good theater, to merchandise our story.

Cost and Timing

I did a quick, back-of-the-envelope calculation on how I would break down the $00,000 budget:

My fee	$ 0,000
Creative fee	$ 0,000
Production fee and third-party cost	$ 0,000
Media	$00,000
Measurement	$ 0,000
Total	$00,000

This clearly doesn't leave much to invest in working media, but given we're confining ourselves to one market, and given we're buying available, pre-emptable DRTV time, I assume the $00,000 will allow us to acquire a reasonable volume of advertising. This is something we will to explore in more detail.

But as I look at the budget, there is an even bigger challenge to address.

As I deconstructed the work to prepare this letter of proposal, I realized there is more to do than I initially envisioned, and I need to answer a number of questions to develop a tighter estimate—for my time, for the time of the people who would work with me, for the third-party costs we would incur, and for the working media dollars we have left to invest.

For example, I need to speak with creative teams to see what they would charge. The same is true with a freelance producer. I also don't know what our voice-over talent will cost (I'm assuming this will be nonunion talent, to avoid ongoing holding and renewal fees). I don't know what it will cost to create the slates. I don't know how much it will cost to modify the spots to obscure the credit card brands, should we go this route. And I don't know how much a recording studio and an editing studio will cost.

To address these questions, I propose we divide the work into two phases. In Phase 1, I will contact creative and production people to get an estimate on their time. I will also explore the various media options and arrive at a recommendation. I will develop a tighter estimate of cost— something we can rely on. I will lay out a production schedule. And I will present all of this in a detailed letter or PowerPoint presentation.

Assuming Phase 1 yields answers you're comfortable with, we'll proceed with Phase 2 and execute the work.

Phase 1 will take about one or two weeks. My fee for this work is $0,000, which is below my standard $000 an hour rate but sufficient to get Phase 1 done and to get you to a sound, well-informed go/no-go decision point.

Next Steps

I realize this letter of proposal has taken you down a path that is different from the one you expected. My apologies for this, but I think it's preferable to raise and address these issues first, before we begin work and prior to committing to a significant investment.

If you decide you want to proceed, you can authorize me to begin work by signing below and returning a copy of this letter to me. I will then issue a $0,000 invoice, which will need to be paid before I present my findings, which means in about a week.

Stepping back from this detail for a minute, this is an incredibly challenging and interesting assignment, and I'd be delighted to partner with you in developing and executing it. But regardless of your decision, I appreciate the opportunity to submit this proposal and look forward to hearing back from you.

I'll follow up with a call later this week. In the meantime, if you have any questions or concerns, or need additional information or clarification, please call me at (000) 000-0000 or email me at *robert@solomonstrategic.com.*

Best regards,

Robert

Robert Solomon
Solomon Strategic

WEBSITE.COM AUTHORIZATION:

_____

Name   Date

The letter proposals you'll write won't sound or look at all like this one, but this should serve as a modest guide you can use to improve your work.

CHAPTER 45

The Zen of PowerPoint

Okay, there's nothing Zen about this; I'm sorry. I struggled for a title, and this was the best I could do.

I'm often reminded of how easy it is to ridicule Power-Point presentations. I recall a *New York Times* article in which the author showed how PowerPoint can dumb down a message as inspiring as Lincoln's Gettysburg address or Martin Luther King's "I have a dream" speech.

No argument here. Badly used, PowerPoint can eviscerate even the most thoughtful content. That said, PowerPoint has its purpose. Account people like it because it is relatively simple to use and quick to fix without the help of an art director or a producer. Plenty of times, I've edited my material just as I was about to go on stage.

But speed and ease also are part of the problem; we're not any good at playing art director, and that's reflected in the slides we proudly put up on the screen.

So how do we make PowerPoint work well? Here are eight suggestions with examples taken from a presentation I give on this book:

1. *Start with a template you create and own.* I'm certainly no master at creating an original template, so this is where I turn to an art director for help. Instead of working in PowerPoint, which is visually limited, the art director first works in Quark or Photoshop to create the template, then imports the result into PowerPoint.

   That's exactly what I did on the presentation that I developed to support this book. Here are the three basic template forms I asked an art director to create for me:

   Template 1

Template 2

Template 3

I used these templates to create the content of my talk: simple, visual, and effective, I think. We don't have the benefit of color in this book, but if we did, you'd see *The Art of Client Service* highlighted in a bright sash of warm red with the book photograph casting a shadow.

2. *If you're confident and the audience is receptive, open with a joke.* If I had to rely on my own material for humor, you'd be walking out the door in the first minute. But if you have *The New Yorker* "cartoon bank" at your disposal, you're on much more solid ground. For about $20, you can start with something at least mildly amusing. Here's what I used:

3. *Keep it short.* My slides work like billboards, cuing me to the right content, helping the audience to follow along. This is about the most material I want to be on a slide:

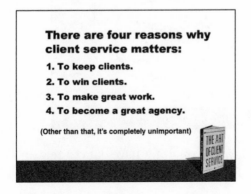

4. *Think in headlines.* This is all I need to prompt a lengthy riff on the importance of integrity in client service:

5. *Be visual.* I was very proud that I could construct this "cocktail napkin" in PowerPoint, which replicates what I include in the book on its last page. It shows, better than mere words could, the key elements of client service:

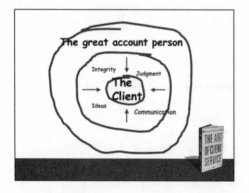

Also, when you don't have data to rely upon, create the appearance of support. Most of what I have to say on the subject of client service is opinion, not fact. But it helps if I can quote an article or two. Here's an example from *Advertising Age:*

6. *"Produce" your slides.* Unfortunately, I can't show you step-by-step how I built the slide below; for that you would need PowerPoint itself operating in "presentation" mode. But PowerPoint has a surprisingly easy and intuitive "slide customization" capability that allows you to add animations, wipes, and sound to what otherwise would be a static image. Here's an example of a fully produced, finished slide. Each one of these images "wipes on" to the page at a mouse click:

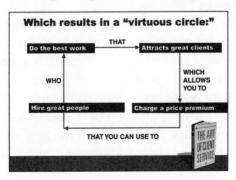

7. *Handwriting helps.* It doesn't take much to scan something written by hand to add some visual interest:

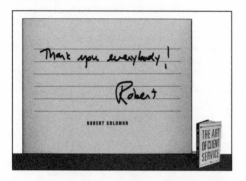

8. *With a presenter or without?* This is the last point—and the most important.

Many of the best presentations serve as visual support for the presenter. In cases like these, PowerPoint should be a prop, not the central focus. But what happens after the presentation, when someone who was not in the room reads the material? They would struggle to fill in the blanks.

Presentations like these must stand on their own, without a speaker. They must tell a story yet still be structured in PowerPoint.

The best way to show you this is to share a full presentation with you. Space prevents this, but if you visit *www.artofclientservice.com,* you can download an example I posted there.

There are books that can help you create effective PowerPoint presentations, but if you follow these eight simple rules, you will master the Zen of PowerPoint and emerge as an enlightened "deck swami."

CHAPTER 46

In a Hi-Tech World,
Be Low-Tech

"On the Internet, nobody knows you're a dog."

I was having lunch with two incredibly talented creative people when the subject of the new edition of this book came up. "It's been four years since your last book, and so much has changed," one of them said. "Are you going to write about how to use technology to serve clients?"

I wasn't planning to talk about technology. But then I realized that I have a cell phone, a BlackBerry, and two email addresses that allow me to be in nearly 24/7 contact with my clients. And it's not at all uncommon for me to respond to client voice mail and answer their emails at midnight.

So I should talk about what having all this hardware and software means. I thought long and hard about it and ultimately came to a startling revelation:

It means almost nothing to a good account person.

Yes, it's great to be in contact. Yes, it's both smart and productive to respond to voice mail and email at all hours of the day. And yes, your clients will no doubt approve of your dedication to their interests.

But there's something almost insidious about having this technology at your disposal. The client service people I know are busier than ever. The easiest thing is to email or late call. Get that task off your plate and move to the next one.

And therein lies the problem. As voice mail and email replace live, in-person contact, you find yourself more in touch but less connected with the people you serve. So in a business that is all about the 21st century when it comes to communicating, I urge you to remain firmly last century. Use hi-tech to help, not replace, face-to-face.

I've got to go now—my BlackBerry is buzzing, and my cell phone is ringing.

CHAPTER 47

Always Think Endgame

The client was wrong. The agency had agreed to create a print ad on a ridiculously tight schedule, with the understanding that we would do our creative presentation on a particular day. Now the client was saying she couldn't meet on the day we agreed to; she wanted to delay a day, but still make all the magazine closings. "You can make up the day in the schedule," she said.

Normally we could. Normally we would be delighted to have an extra day to develop creative concepts. But this schedule wasn't normal. It was broken down into hours, not days. A day lost was a big deal. It threatened to blow our closing dates.

We could have insisted on holding to the original schedule. We could have won the argument, but we would have lost in the end.

The client would remember. The next time we needed her to be flexible on a date, I could see her pointing to the schedule, then pointing to me and saying, "This is what you committed to, so don't even think about asking for an extra hour, let alone an extra day."

So we figured out how to make the publication closings even with the one-day delay on the creative presentation. The message: Working with clients and colleagues is a never-ending process of negotiation and compromise. Always think endgame. Remember that an argument won can become an account lost.

CHAPTER 48

No Surprises about
Money or Time

After I took over running a major account at one of the agencies I worked for, I discovered the agency had, during a period of seven months, exceeded the agreed-on fee budget by nearly $1 million (yes, $1 million). The client/agency relationship had been rocky, and the previous leadership on the account chose not to disclose the fee overrun to the client, fearing it would jeopardize the account.

I inherited this problem knowing that a cardinal rule of account service is to never surprise your clients about a cost overrun or a scheduling delay. But I had the advantage of being the new guy on the account. I investigated the cost overrun. It appeared that roughly half of it was due to agency inefficiency, the other half due to excessive client changes and unbudgeted additional assignments.

When the client made revisions to the work and added assignments, the agency of course should have adjusted its budgets and secured client approval for the higher fees. The agency, fearing for the future of the account, failed to do this. Over time, as the problem grew larger and larger, it became increasingly difficult to address. Rather than bringing up the issue with the client, the account team ignored it. When the agency's accounting department pressed the account team to speak with the client, the account people responded, "If we do, we'll lose the account!"

I told my management that I was going to settle the issue without delay. I prepared them to expect nothing better than half of the $1 million overage. Then I went to see the client. I took her through the problem, apologized for the agency's failure to disclose it, offered to have the agency absorb half the overage, and assured them it would never happen again.

Instead of being angry, which she had every right to be, and instead of firing the agency on the spot, which she easily could have done, the client accepted my apology and my solution. We went on to have a very productive relationship for years thereafter.

This was a problem not of my own making, but even so, I vowed I would never be placed in that position again. I made a commitment to myself that I would always advise clients up front about the cost and timing implications of their decisions, so they could make fully informed decisions.

When a client calls with a change or a request, it can make you feel a little uncomfortable to say, "Let me figure out what the change will cost and if it will have an impact on the schedule, then get right back to you."

But you owe it to your clients, and to your agency, to do exactly that. By doing so, you avoid the perils of "scope creep," when a project grows beyond what initially was planned. And you avoid any after-the-fact surprises that result in painful consequences, ranging from a loss of money, to a loss of trust, to a lost account.

CHAPTER 49

Deal with Trouble Head-On

Advertising is people intensive. Given the number of hands that touch even the simplest assignment, it is astonishing how much work gets produced error-free.

Still, things get derailed; on occasion, there is a full-scale train wreck. A deadline gets blown. There is a mistake in a print ad. The wrong commercial gets shipped.

When something goes awry, get to your client with a full explanation of what happened and why. Whenever possible, be prepared to outline one or more ways to address the problem. Move quickly; you want to deliver the bad news to the clients. You don't want them to hear it from another source.

If the agency is on the hook for serious money, get senior management involved immediately and work out what you are prepared to do financially before you call the client. Volunteer the financial solution before the client asks for it.

Above all, never, ever lie to your client. Sure you might get away with it this time. At some point, though, you won't. Once you're caught in a lie, your single greatest asset—your credibility—will be gone forever.

CHAPTER 50

If Things Go Wrong,
Take the Blame

Steve Gardner, president of Gardner Nelson & Partners, says, "The best account people have such a profound sense of responsibility that they literally find a way to blame themselves for anything that goes wrong." He's right, and that's the way it should be.

Years ago an agency creative director and I had lunch with a trade publication reporter. The reporter asked about the work we were doing for one client. The creative director explained that we were working on a new product launch for that client. The reporter took note, and a couple of days later the published story on our agency included a reference to the client's product launch.

There was just one small problem: The client had not announced the new product yet.

The client was furious when he called me. He demanded to know how the agency could be so stupid. I explained it was my fault. I didn't say anything about the creative director spilling the news. As far as I was concerned, it was my job to make sure the creative director didn't reveal anything confidential. I wasn't the author of the mistake, but I didn't think twice about taking ownership of it.

You provide air cover for everyone in the agency. If something goes wrong in media, in creative, in production, then it happened on your watch. You are responsible. Take ownership, and be prepared to take the heat from the client.

CHAPTER 51

What Happens
When I Screw Up?

A little earlier in this book, I said that when working with clients, there should be absolutely no surprises about money or time. You'll recall that I rode in on the proverbial white horse to rescue my agency from a very difficult financial situation. My solution was actually quite simple—split the dollar difference and learn a lesson—but it saved the agency, and it kept our client. I was pretty proud of myself for being so wise and resourceful.

But enough about this rare occasion of personal competence. Let's talk instead about a more frequent example of when I screwed up.

The story begins innocently enough. I wrote a direct mail recommendation for a client that included a rough cost estimate and a projected mail quantity. I developed the estimate on a fairly logical set of assumptions based on my years of experience, and I felt I was safe with the number.

My client liked what I presented and gave us approval to proceed. I wrote a creative brief, confirmed a schedule, and met with the creative team. After some back-and-forth with the writer, art director, and creative director, we arrived at a couple of ideas we liked. We took them to the client. And after a few more back-and-forths, we arrived at a plan that pleased all of us.

I then wrote detailed specifications for the idea and put the job out to bid.

The numbers came back. We were over budget. Not by 10 percent, or even 20 percent, which I might have been able to defend. No, as I added up the costs, it became clear that we were over by more than twice what I had estimated earlier. Yes, that's right: the actual cost was more than twice what I had said the work would cost.

These were not hourly fees that we could absorb, which would be bad enough; these were hard costs due to third parties. It's a good thing the windows didn't open, because I might have been inclined to jump.

Because jumping was out, I needed another solution. I thought about revising or eliminating some of the pieces that would go in the package. But in the end, it became clear only one thing would truly make an impact: cut the mailing quantity.

I asked our printer to refigure the package at 50 percent of the original press run. To my eternal relief, the numbers came back nearly on target. And although the final mailing would be half the initial estimate, it still would be larger and more ambitious than anything the client had previously attempted. That at least was one positive note in an otherwise grim reality.

Now all I had to do was to sell this to the client, but there was one complicating factor: I was scheduled to go out of town the following week, and I wouldn't be able to speak with him face-to-face. No problem, I thought—I'll write him an email (remember Chapter 46?).

Over the weekend, I wrote a long, meticulously detailed analysis of the problem, described the various solutions I explored, then offered the solution. Before I pressed "send," I wanted another opinion, so I emailed the document to a colleague for a comment. He wrote back: "You cannot send this email. This problem is too serious, and the solution too complicated, for email. It needs a 'live' discussion."

He was right of course; it was if he had read my book and I hadn't. I thought about it for a minute, and although it was Saturday, decided to reschedule my out-of-town meeting. I then wrote to my client and scheduled a meeting on Monday.

On Monday, I took him through the whole situation: the source of the problem, the possible solutions, and the recommendation. I admit I cringed when he said, "You are actually double the budget? How can that possibly, possibly be?" But without further complaint, with no invective, and to his eternal credit, he focused on the problem. He was largely responsible for our working out something satisfactory. It wasn't a happy meeting, but we got done what we needed to get done.

Now I could say this outcome would have been very different had I not gotten to know this client well and had I not developed a measure of trust and mutual respect along the way. But that's not what I'm going to say.

I've been in this business for nearly 30 years and certainly knew better, and yet I still managed to screw up big-time.

The lesson? Do not assume anything, and never, ever be as glib or as cavalier as I was about money. Check and recheck your claims, then check them again. Above all, remember your own advice. And by God, follow it.

CHAPTER 52

Remember the Personal Side of Business Relationships

I was only five minutes late for the client dinner. When I arrived, I found everyone seated. A place was left for me at the end of the table. Nothing wrong with that, except . . .

Except that I was seated next to agency colleagues, not clients. The clients were at the other end of a long table. I had to shout my greeting to them.

This was not what I expected. What I expected was a well-orchestrated seating arrangement. Because there were no place cards to direct people, seating became an ad hoc affair, clients sitting with clients, and agency people also bunched together. A primary purpose of any client/agency dinner is to get to know one another better. The best way to ensure this is to intersperse client and agency people, with attention paid to specific pairings.

I made the best of a less-than-optimal situation. From my end-of-the-table perch, I offered a toast to recognize a successful year of partnership, and to wish for many more holiday celebrations together. I conducted an impromptu wine tasting. When a moment presented itself to switch seats, I did, so I could talk with a couple of clients.

The evening was lovely; we all enjoyed ourselves. But for me it was a missed opportunity to get to know the clients better.

If you're responsible for conducting a social event with your client, make sure you take it as seriously as any business meeting. Make sure you plan every detail, to ensure you get the maximum benefit from the event.

If you have clients coming from out of town, meet their plane personally. If you work in a city where that is impractical—New York, Chicago, or LA—have a reliable car service, one you know well, meet and bring them to your office. Ask the car service to send a sedan, not a stretch (it's business, not the prom).

Before your client visits, offer to make hotel reservations, or at least offer suggestions of good hotels, consistent with the client's travel budget and policies, conveniently located near to the agency. Once you know where the client is staying, call the hotel's front desk manager to see if you can arrange a complimentary room upgrade.

Then call the concierge to arrange to have an amenity placed in their room prior to arrival. It could be flowers, a bottle of mineral water, a bowl of fresh fruit, or all of these. Include a welcome note from the agency. The client will appreciate and be impressed by this small gesture.

Arrange for transportation to and from the hotel to the agency. Also arrange to have the car service take the client back to the airport at the conclusion of the visit.

Ask your client to have dinner with you, either the night before the meeting or the evening after its conclusion. Assuming the client says yes, choose a restaurant that you know well, that will make your client feel both comfortable and special, and is quiet enough to conduct a conversation. You need to know your client's tastes, preferences, and special needs. A casual and unintimidating place, or a temple of fine dining? A classic experience, or the latest hot spot?

Cast the dinner with care. Whom do the clients know and like? Whom do they need to meet, or get to know better? Who is good with clients at these events?

Generally follow the rule of having no more than two agency people for every client person in attendance. You want the agency people to focus on the client, not on each other. The 2:1 maximum ratio ensures that; 1:1 is even better. Besides, more than two agency people per client makes the dinner look like a boondoggle. That's not the impression you want to make on your clients, your colleagues, or your management.

A small group is better for business discussion; a large group is better for pure fun. Fun is good; fun is a legitimate client-dinner objective. You want the clients to enjoy the experience, and it's great if you and your team enjoy it as well.

If it's a large group, use place cards so you can orchestrate a seating arrangement that meets your business needs. You might want the client to get to know certain people; you might want certain team members seated next to certain clients because you think they'll connect on a personal level.

In advance of the dinner, arrange a special menu and have printed copies at each place at the table. This simplifies the evening, makes it feel more special, plus removes prices from view, which is a nice touch.

Talk to the restaurant manager about where the group will be placed in the dining room. It might be preferable to select a restaurant that has a private dining room. On the other hand, the buzz of the main dining room might be more enjoyable.

Run any dinner, large or small, as you would a meeting. Arrive ahead of your clients or with them. Start on time. Act as the host; oversee the conversation, but do not dominate it. Keep every client engaged.

Keep it lively: Conduct a wine or beer tasting, share some appetizers, have the chef talk about the menu, make some toasts. Do whatever is appropriate for the occasion.

Handle the bill in advance, so you don't have to deal with it at the end of the evening, in front of the clients.

Remember that the dinner, while social, is still a business event. Watch what you drink. Keep an eye and ear open for cues from your clients, spoken or nonverbal. End the evening early if you are meeting the following morning or if the clients are leaving early—unless, of course, the clients want to continue the party. If that's the case, have an after-dinner destination in mind. If it's a group of young clients, it might be a dance club. If the clients are older, maybe a jazz club.

Make sure your clients get back to their hotel safely. Arrange for a car service; escort them if necessary.

Call each client the following day. Tell them how much you appreciate their spending the evening with the agency. Let them know you and your colleagues had a good time. Reinforce the message in a handwritten note to each client.

Then remember to thank your colleagues for joining you. For them, no matter how enjoyable the evening was, it still was an evening away from their family and friends. It still was business.

CHAPTER 53

Take On the Coloration of Your Clients, But Do Not Compromise Your Character

Some of my clients seem to live for golf; they don't just play it, they breathe it. I don't play golf, but I can talk it. I make a point to read the sports reporting on major golf tournaments. That way, if my clients want to talk about how Tiger Woods blew up at the British Open, I'll be ready.

I'm also ready to talk about the latest movie, the hottest Broadway show, or some new restaurant everyone is raving about. From bowling to Beethoven, it doesn't matter. If you're going to be good at account work, you need to be interested in whatever your client is interested in. That means being a voracious consumer of popular culture, and at least on passing terms with higher-brow pursuits.

You also need to be wise enough to sidestep discussions of politics, religion, or controversial subjects best avoided. No matter how friendly you become, remember that clients are still clients, not friends, and edit yourself accordingly.

Client service requires you to be flexible, openminded, and able to handle the unexpected with grace. It also requires you to never compromise your integrity, honesty, or sense of fairness.

Be a good listener. Take a sincere interest in your clients' lives—professionally and personally—while remaining respectful of their privacy. Don't force the relationship; take the time needed to build a personal connection.

I worked with two clients for more than a year and got to know them fairly well. We had more than the occasional lunch together. One day, after finishing up a meeting, I suggested the three of us continue the discussion over dinner. Then I remembered that each had a young child. I was a single guy at the time with not much interest in children, but that didn't stop me from suggesting we bring the kids with us.

The five of us went out for pizza. It was as much fun as I've had at any client dinner, and it was a great way to bond with my clients. Every time thereafter, I could ask about their boys by name.

It was a great lesson in taking on the coloration of my clients.

CHAPTER 54

No Matter How Social It Becomes, Never Forget That It's Business

I once had one martini too many (two actually, which for a lightweight like me is one too many) over dinner with a client. I wound up saying something I shouldn't have said. Fortunately for me, and my agency, there was no damage as a result. But I learned an important lesson about self-restraint.

If you work with clients long enough, you usually have an opportunity to spend time with them outside the office. There's the occasional lunch or dinner. You might play golf or tennis together, or go to a ballgame. These are good things to do. Spending time away from work allows you to talk about work in a different context. You can use such occasions not only to be social, but also to deal with tough issues.

No matter how many dinners you attend, no matter how friendly you become with your client, never mistake your relationship for personal friendship. Never forget that the person sitting across from you is always your client.

So watch what you drink, watch how you behave, and watch what you say. No tales out of school, no alcohol talking.

CHAPTER 55

Once a Client, Always a Client

I had lunch the other day with a client. Not a current client; I haven't worked with this individual in more than a decade. But I've made it a point to stay in touch. After all these years, it's looking pretty unlikely that we'll ever get to work together again. It doesn't matter.

Once a client and I are no longer working together, I don't decide to stay in touch based on how likely that client is to run a big account again. My view is that once you've been my client, you'll always be my client.

If you're my client and are open to staying in contact after we're no longer working together, I'll make sure we do. If there's a way I can be of help, I'll do my best.

That client whom I had lunch with is now a friend. He's served as a job reference. He's recommended me to possible clients and potential employers. I've done the same for him. As I said, he's not likely to be my client again, but it doesn't matter.

PART THREE

Style and Substance

"Jenkins, I think you've taken our casual dress policy a bit too far."

Make an Investment
in Your Personal Style

Early in my career, I worked for a very smart, very personable, and outrageously funny executive. He was a big guy, kind of a bowling ball with legs. A client described him as "an unmade waterbed." That moniker captured his rumpled, shirttail-out, tie-askew style.

He could pull this off because of his outsized personality and big brain. It wouldn't work for most other people, and even if it did, I wouldn't recommend it.

That's because you are the agency's lead representative to your client, the manifestation of the agency's brand and culture. So regardless if the style you cultivate is Chicago conservative, New York downtown hip, or San Francisco laid-back, grooming counts. It affects how others see you and how they judge you professionally. It can affect how you feel about yourself.

I suggest you do what it takes to get the styling details right, from a decent haircut to a decent pair of shoes, to everything in between. It's more about investing time and attention than dollars and cents. It's a matter of taste. I know guys who wear expensive suits and still manage to look disheveled. I know other guys who wear a sport shirt and jeans and look completely pulled together. I know women who spend a fortune on clothes but don't get the look right. I know other women who bargain basement shop and look terrific.

After years of increasing *casualization* of corporate dress, there has been a shift back toward business suits, for both men and women. Yet business casual is far from dead. If anything, the rules, if there are any rules, are more confusing than ever. Do you wear a suit? When is casual okay? What exactly is meant by *casual*?

Your agency probably has a style; it might even have a dress code. If that's the case, take your cues from what you see or what the rules say. If not, here are a few suggestions.

- *If you're meeting with a client, adapt the client's dress code.* For example, if your client wears khakis, you can do the same, but take it up a notch. Instead of wearing a polo shirt, put on a dress shirt, and add a sport coat. Wear a great pair of loafers. Add a cool watch. Carry a good briefcase. Women can wear a blouse and skirt, a sweater and slacks, or anything else a notch above casual, instead of a suit.

- Casual *is not code for slovenly.* If you're not meeting with clients and the agency is a dress-casual place, then dress casually, but don't take casual too far. Plus, keep a dress shirt or blouse in your office, in case you have to meet with a client unexpectedly.

- *You can push casual a bit further in the summer.* When it's really hot, get rid of the jacket, unless you have to have one to meet with your client.

- *Think about wearing a suit, but dress it down a bit.* No tie. Maybe a sport shirt or sweater rather than a dress shirt or blouse. Hipper shoes rather than wingtips or pumps.

- *Suede is great.* If you wear leather shoes, you have to keep them polished. Suede shoes take a minute to brush; no polishing required.

- *Invest in a few suits that are the best you can afford.* It's better to have a few well-tailored items than more items of lower quality. They will fit you better and will last longer. That means staying away from trendy, highly perishable design, fabrics, and patterns, and instead gravitating toward classic design in muted fabrics and patterns. If you get bored with the same three or four suits in your wardrobe, don't buy another suit. Buy a new shirt or tie, or blouse, to change the look.

- *If your client is out of town, or if you have to travel, buy clothes that travel.* For example, in suits, crepe wool is great. It holds its shape, resists wrinkles, and packs well.

- *Ask for style help if you need it.* Take a long look in the mirror. If you don't have what it takes to style yourself, admit it and find some help. I have a colleague in the business who always looks great. He didn't have a clue on how to dress, but he was smart enough to enlist the help of a friend who does. Now he never shops alone.

- *Think in terms of a uniform.* Men have done this for years, and so have some women I know. For men, the uniform used to be a pinstripe suit, white shirt, stripped tie, wingtip shoes. That's not the uniform I'd suggest for most agency people, but the concept makes sense. It allows you to mix and match various pieces in your wardrobe. It allows you to work with fewer items, which allows you to invest a little more in each piece. It makes packing for travel easier. Lots of New Yorkers have made black their uniform color. They can get dressed in the dark. Not that black isn't cool, but you don't have to be quite so strict, or so somber. Confining your business wardrobe to just a few colors—black, blue, and gray, for example—does make dressing easier.

Style won't make or break your career. There are dozens of successful account people who don't have a clue about fashion. There are others who know how to dress, but that's all they know (the classic "empty suit"). Still, it's a competitive world, and you need every edge you can get. Looking good is just one more detail in a business that is all about details. So why not get this one right? It just might make a difference.

CHAPTER 57

Invest Some Time (Again) in These Books

Four years ago, when I compiled my list of 15 books that every account person should read, I asked myself, "Will these books endure?" At the time, I had no idea I would be sitting down today to revisit the list to see what I could discard and what I could add.

The good news: All 15 books passed the endurance test. In fairness, some—like David Ogilvy's or Strunk and White's—had passed the test well before I recommended them. But the jury was still out on others, like *The Tipping Point* or *The Do-It-Yourself Lobotomy*. But even these newer books remain as powerful and relevant today as they were years ago.

The bad news: There are too many books! In the last four years, I don't know how many hundreds of titles have appeared on the market, many of them truly worthy of inclusion. But my initial premise remains: to give you a short list of books, not an interminable one.

My way of dealing with this is twofold:

1. I'm going to kind of punt by recommending you read two *Adweek* articles by agency hero Tom Messner. Tom wrote "The New Testament" on December 12, 2005, and "The Old Testament" on January 16, 2006. In "The New Testament," Tom wrote about a wide range of terrific recent books that had little overlap with my list. In "The Old Testament," he wrote about the classics, a few of which appear here. But together, these lists make for interesting bedtime reading, and I encourage you to seek them out.

2. I've selected five new books to add to my earlier list. The selection is admittedly imperfect, and I'm certain you could do as well or better with your own picks.

That said, and in no particular order, my five choices follow:

1. Malcolm Gladwell made the list with his first book, *The Tipping Point*. He makes the list again with his second book, *Blink*. He's so smart and writes so well that I've no doubt that when he publishes his third book, it will make the list, too. He's that good.

2. One of the notable omissions in the previous book list was in media. Fortunately, David Verklin came to the rescue. Even if he wasn't the author of this book's introduction, I'd happily recommend *Watch This Listen Up Click Here,* which he wrote with Bernice Kanner. It's a terrific way to make sense of the ongoing media revolution.

3. You should read Marty Neumeier's *The Brand Gap* for the sheer pleasure of experiencing a book written by an amazing visual thinker. It offers a unified definition of what a brand is, and I admire the ambition inherent in that argument.

4. I suppose *Juicing the Orange* could be viewed as one long advertisement for the Fallon agency. But even if it is, who cares? The stories are great, and authors Pat Fallon and Fred Senn display unusual candor and humor in revisiting some of the agency's best work. Of all the new books on creative, this one stands out.

5. Choosing a fifth and final book posed the biggest challenge. I thought of Douglas Atkins's book, *The Culting of Brands,* which a client recommended. Jon Steel's *Perfect Pitch* also came to mind, as did Erich Joachimshtaler's *Hidden in Plain Sight,* which talks about seeking simplicity in looking for a client's next big idea. But most of these are on Messner's list, and that was good enough for me. In the end, I looked back, not forward, to Tom Kelley's *The Art of Innovation,* published in 2001. I chose it because it's not about advertising—it is about how to create new products—and because it is about how to encourage a culture of creativity. Kelley talks at length about his firm Ideo, and all I can say is that I wish I was creative enough to work there.

So there you have it: 5 new books to add to the list of 15.

ON COMMUNICATING

1. Strunk, William, and E. B. White. *The Elements of Style,* 4th ed. (Allyn & Bacon, 2000).

2. Zinsser, William. *On Writing Well,* 6th ed. (Harper-Perennial, 1998).

3. Roman, Kenneth, and Joel Raphaelson. *Writing That Works* (Quill/HarperCollins, 2000).

4. Hoff, Ron. *I Can See You Naked* (Andrews and McNeel, 1992).

ON CLIENT RELATIONSHIPS

5. Maister, David H., Charles H. Green, and Robert M. Galford. *The Trusted Advisor* (Free Press, 2000).

6. Sheth, Jagdish, and Andrew Sobel. *Clients for Life* (Simon & Schuster, 2000).

7. Solomon, Robert. *The Art of Client Service* (Kaplan Publishing, 2008).

ON CREATIVITY AND ADVERTISING

8. Monahan, Tom. *The Do-It-Yourself Lobotomy* (John Wiley & Sons, 2002).

9. Sullivan, Luke. *Hey Whipple, Squeeze This* (John Wiley & Sons, 1998).

10. Ogilvy, David. *Ogilvy on Advertising* (Vintage Books, 1985).

ON STRATEGY

11. Ries, Al, and Jack Trout. *Positioning: The Battle for Your Mind* (McGraw-Hill Trade, 2000).

12. Morgan, Adam. *Eating the Big Fish* (John Wiley & Sons, 1999).

13. Steel, Jon. *Truth, Lies, and Advertising* (John Wiley & Sons, 1998).

14. Gladwell, Malcolm. *The Tipping Point* (Little, Brown & Company, 2000).

ON BUSINESS LEADERSHIP

15. Collins, Jim. *Good to Great* (HarperBusiness, 2001).

FIVE NEW BOOKS

16. Fallon, Pat, and Fed Senn. *Juicing the Orange* (Boston: Harvard Business School Press, 2006).

17. Gladwell, Malcolm. *Blink: The Power of Thinking Without Thinking* (Boston: Little, Brown and Company, 2005).

18. Kelley, Tom, and Jonathan Littman. *The Art of Innovation* (New York: Doubleday, 2001).

19. Neumeier, Marty. *The Brand Gap: How to Bridge the Distance Between Business Strategy and Design* (Indianapolis, IN: New Riders, 2006).

20. Verklin, David, and Bernice Kanner. *Watch This Listen Up Click Here* (Hoboken, NJ: John Wiley & Sons, 2007).

One more thing . . .

CHAPTER **58**

Remember to Say
"Thank You"

It's amazing how much power those two words have. A simple thank you—to colleagues for their assistance, to clients for their business—should be a given. Yet it often is not. People assume that others know they are grateful. Account people in particular shouldn't fall into that trap. Go out of your way to say thanks, for the smallest favor, for the biggest help, and for anything in between.

I worked for one agency boss who was one of the most demanding people I ever met. People always seemed willing to go the extra mile for him, though. There were lots of reasons, but I'm convinced one of them was that he regularly acknowledged the contributions of his staff.

He would leave a voicemail message, or send a handwritten note. If you did something special, you'd find flowers on your desk the following morning, or a gift certificate. It really wasn't just the magnitude of his gestures that mattered; it simply was that he *made* them.

People I know still speak with affection about this boss, even when they have something critical to say about him.

I worked for another agency boss who almost never thanked her people for their efforts. People didn't go the extra mile for this boss, at least not willingly. They generally expressed anger, not affection, for her. She just didn't get it. It was if she found it embarrassing or awkward to show appreciation for the work of her staff. I once remember being astonished at a rare "thank you" call from her. I hadn't received such a call from her in years.

I don't think a day goes by without my writing a hand-written note or an e-mail to someone, to say "thanks for the help," or "I appreciate the quick turn-around," or something similar. I also stop by people's offices to say thanks in person. I call clients to do the same. It takes so little effort, and it delivers so much benefit. It feels good to say thank you. People appreciate being acknowledged. And it makes it easier to be critical or demanding when you need to be.

The longest section of *Brain Surgery for Suits* was my acknowledgments section. I recognized by name 92 colleagues, clients, friends, and family members, and I'm certain I could have doubled the list and still not included everyone who deserved to be acknowledged. I won't subject you to a list of that length, but I do want to thank some groups of people and a few individuals.

To all my colleagues, clients, and friends in the business, you have my deepest appreciation for all you've shared with me, and all you've taught me these many years. To the agency executives who helped me with the account person's reading list, thank you for your thoughtful contributions, and your encouragement as I struggled with this book.

My agent, Jim Donovan, deserves more credit than I can offer for his terrific advice and steadfast support. My editor at Kaplan, Shannon Berning, was also terrifically supportive, as were Joshua Martino and Dominique Polfliet. I want to thank Tom Nelson and Jaydee Jana for their cover design. I especially want to thank David Verklin for his thoughtful Foreword to the book.

The person I want to thank most of all is my wife Roberta, who remains the soul of my life.

What Makes a Great Account Person?

"I got tired of being called a suit."

I was interviewing a candidate for an entry-level assistant account executive's position. She was fresh out of college, her work experience was limited to summer jobs and internships, but she was smart, aggressive, funny, and self-confident. For some reason that eluded me, she wanted to be an account person. I figured I might be working for her in ten years.

After questioning this promising young person about everything from why she chose to study history in college to what she was currently reading, I asked if she had any questions for me. She replied, "I have only one." I figured she would ask me about the agency's goals, how I became such a self-important success, or something else grand and sweeping of that nature. But she surprised me.

"What makes a great account person?" she asked.

Simple question. Complicated answer. If you put this to 100 people in advertising, you would get 100 different answers.

Here's what I told her:

It's more about skills and qualities than about education and experience. A degree in literature or philosophy might be more valuable than an MBA. Tending bar will teach you more than will working in a company that has no clue about collaboration or client service.

It used to be that agencies would train their account people extensively. These days that's increasingly rare. The training is shorter and less complete, and fewer agencies invest in it. But that doesn't place a set of handcuffs on you. Just because agencies don't teach doesn't mean you can't learn. You simply have to take greater responsibility for your own on-the-job training. Agencies offer plenty of opportunity for that, if you're willing to invest the time and effort. It might be between midnight and 8:00 AM; it might be on Saturday and Sunday. If you want to learn, that's just what it might take.

Speaking of nights and weekends, new business is one of the best places to learn. In new business the agency moves at warp speed, ideas are the currency you trade in, and some of the agency's smartest and most senior people inevitably are assigned to work on the pitch. Volunteer to help. You'll have to work nights and weekends on top of the nights and weekends you're already working. All you might get to do is fold, collate, and staple, but you will get to observe. You will get to interact with senior people. You'll get to see them tackle a tough marketing challenge and how they solve it. If you're lucky, you'll get to participate in some small way in helping the agency win. You'll feel some of the heat that gets generated by one of these things.

Now what about skills? Communication is at the top of the list, both written and oral. You've got to be good on paper. An agency might teach you to write a conference report, a creative brief, a point-of-view letter, a strategy deck, or at least show you examples that you can use as "go-bys." What the agency won't teach, shouldn't have to teach, is concision and clarity, style and organization. These you must develop yourself. Start by reading William Strunk and E. B. White's *The Elements of Style* and William Zinsser's *On Writing Well.* Follow what they say and, no matter how good (or bad) your writing is, it will get better.

You also have to be good on your feet—in meetings, on the phone, in presentations, over dinner, or wherever else you connect with clients and colleagues. You can learn to be a competent presenter at an agency; you'll probably have the chance to present to your colleagues and your boss, if not your clients. If you work at it, if you practice, if you have an instinct for it, you just might become good enough to bring tears to the eyes of your audience.

No one is going to teach you to be good in the moment, to know what to say and just how to say it. No one is going to teach you what not to say, and when it's smart to hold your tongue.

Communicating isn't just about what you say, it's about listening and really hearing what the other person says. It's about the ability to interpret the subtext, not just the text, of any communication.

When it comes to skills, communication is the one every account executive must master.

There is one other skill that separates good account people from great account people: the ability to generate ideas. Many good account people have great integrity and solid judgment. They are masters of their discipline, communicate well, are good with clients, supportive of colleagues, and excellent at process. They may rise to very senior levels in their agencies, even to CEO. But if they are not idea generators, they fall short of being great.

Ideas are the blood and bone of advertising and marketing. Any competent agency can make an ad, but great agencies make ads fueled by invention, driven by ideas. Likewise, any competent account person can run a piece of business, but great account people can grow a piece of business by bringing ideas to clients that solve problems and capitalize on opportunities.

There are other things that matter—good quantitative and analytical capabilities, an orientation to organization and detail—but nothing matters more than the ability to communicate well and the ability to generate ideas. Ideas, and the ability to communicate them effectively, distinguish great account people from good.

When it comes to qualities, there are two that stand above all others: integrity and judgment.

Integrity has always been an essential quality of the best account people, but in the wake of recent business scandals, it has become even more critical. Integrity is key to building trust with clients and colleagues. Judgment is key to arriving at the right decision when the circumstances are less than completely clear.

Account people need integrity and judgment in abundance to navigate what are increasingly complex issues and relationships that characterize the advertising and marketing communications business. The high-integrity account person takes ownership of problems. The high-judgment account person has the ability to resolve them fairly for all parties.

Great account people embody other qualities: patience, discipline, grace under pressure, a sense of humor, meticulousness, a sense of ownership, a spirit of collaboration, self-effacement, a sense of context, a service orientation. All of these are incredibly important.

Without patience, you have no hope of dealing with difficult clients and wayward colleagues.

Without discipline, you will never be able to focus on the task at hand.

Without grace under pressure, you will crumble under pressure. There is pressure in our business. At times it is intense.

Without a sense of humor, you will be unable to see that what we do is not brain surgery, and that we are not looking for a cure for cancer. We do advertising; it's critically important to our clients, but it is not a life or death matter.

Without meticulousness, you will make mistakes, and not catch the mistakes of others. An accumulation of small errors can undermine a client relationship.

Without a sense of ownership, you will not take full responsibility for delivering for your clients, and you will not step up when things go wrong. Your colleagues won't respect you, and your clients won't trust you.

Without a spirit of collaboration, you will be unable to marshal the full resources of the agency to the benefit of the client.

Without self-effacement, you will be dissatisfied with the lack of recognition account people receive.

Without a sense of context, you will see the details but not the larger purpose they serve.

Without a service orientation, you have no hope of helping your colleagues and clients achieve their goals.

With that I paused. I wondered if the candidate sitting across from me was sorry she asked. No question I got a little carried away with my answer, but she seemed to be still with me. She was a good listener, and she was patient.

I concluded my monologue by saying that if I were to reduce this to four guiding principles, they would be integrity and judgment, communication and ideas. Then I grabbed a piece of paper and drew this sketch:

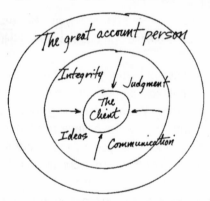

"Does any of this make sense?" I asked.

"All of it," she replied. "Maybe I should be a copywriter." I laughed. But she must have heard me, because today she runs an agency.

"Let me see the first one again."

Accountability, 139–40
Account managers, xii
Account person, what
  makes great, 169–75
Account planning, 22
Advertising, xii, xxi,
  xxiii–xxvi, 164
    format, 12–13
    measurement, 118
    production, 118
Adweek, 162
Agency
  recommendation,
    44
  spokesperson, 45
Agenda, 79–80
Agreements, 111
Almco, 49
Ammirati Puris Lintas,
  xvi, xix, xxvi–xxvii, 27,
  31, 89, 97
Annual report, 30
Argument holes, 59
Arrogance, 76
Art director, 27, 28
Art of Innovation, The, 163
Assignment
  ownership, 28
  recap, 112, 114–15
  start, 3–5
Atkin, Douglas, 163
Audience, 21
Audit trail, 85

Background material,
  71–72
Banking, xxiii–xxiv

Barriers, 105–6
BBDO, xxvii, 97
Beethoven, 150
Betting, 5
Billboard slides, 125
BlackBerry, 130, 131
Blame taking, 139–40
Blink, xxv, 162
BMW, xxvii, 97
Bonding, 95–96
Books, 161–65
Brain Surgery for Suits, xi,
  xx, xxii, 167
Brand
  advertising, 7
  living client's, 8–10
  positioning, 25–26
  research, 8–10
Brand Gap, The, 163
Brevity, 24, 81
Bridges, 105–6
Brief, 20–24
  amnesia, 32–33, 34
  client input,
    approval of,
    32–34
  creation, 27–28
  development, 32–34
  outline, 23
British Open, 150
Broadway show, 150
Brokering solutions,
  102–5
Budget, 11–15, 134–36
  estimate, 112, 119–20
  overage, 140–44
Business casual, 158

Cable, 6
Carat Americas, xii, xiii,
  xx
Carat Management
  Conference, xiii
Casualization, 158
Celebrity spokesperson,
  73
Cell phone, 130, 131
Charles Schwab, xxvii,
  97
Checklist, 72
Choices, 109
Clarity, 82
Client
  contact, 154
  customers, 29
  fighting for work
    with, 46–48
  involvement, 51–52
  offices, 29
  personally knowing,
    30
  perspective of, 29–31
  presentation, 40,
    57–59
  service matters, xiv,
    xxi, xxvi–xxviii
  signature, 33
  visitation, 93–94
Client/agency
  dinner, 145–46
  relationships, 97–99
Closure, 84
Collaboration, 49–50,
  51–52, 63–64,
  100–101, 174

Colleague
  fighting about work
    with, 46–48
  solidarity, 35–36
Coloration, of clients,
  150–51
Commitment, 98, 102–4,
  105
Communication, xxi,
  130–31, 164, 171–72,
  174, 175
Company
  goals, 4
  history, 9
Compaq Computer, 49
Competition, 21, 30, 101
Competitive analysis, 26
Competitive landscape,
  30
Comp interpretation, 18
Compromise, 132–33
Concept, 16–17, 18
  choices, number of,
    43–45
Consistency, xx-xxi
Consultation, 102–4,
  105
Context sense, 174
Continental Congress,
  100
Controversial subjects,
  150–51
Conversational writing,
  112
Copy revisions, 13
Cost overrun, 134–36
Creative brief, 72
  outline, 23
Creative directors,
  91–92
Creative team partners,
  27–28
Creative work, 115–16
Creativity, 164
Credibility, 104, 138

Credit, distribution of,
  91–92
CRM. *See* Customer
  relationship marketing
Culting of Brands, The, 163
Customer
  being, 31
  engagement, 37
  research, 26
Customer relationship
  marketing (CRM), 6

Declaration of
  Independence, 100
Design Communications
  Group, xvi–xvii
Deutsch, xxvii, 97
Digitas, xvi
Dinner
  arrangements,
    147–48
  menu, 148
Diplomacy, 55
Direct marketing, xix
Discipline, 173
Doctor-patient
  relationship, xxv–xxvi
Do-It-Yourself Lobotomy,
  The, 161
Dominating, 82–83
Doublechecking
  elements, 140–44
Dress code, 158–59
Dressing down, 159
Drinking, 148

Effective
  communication, 76
Elements of Style, xxii, 171
Email, 143
  addresses, 130
  conference report,
    85
Emotional commitment,
  54

Emotional detachment,
  54–55
Ethics, 96
Execution, 17, 108, 109
Exit interview, xxiv–xxv
Expectation management,
  16–19, 98

Facts, 107
Fallon, Pat, xxvii, 163
Fallon Worldwide, xxvii,
  163
False starts, avoiding, 52
Federal Express, 31
Feedback, 53–54, 55
Fiduciary responsibility,
  96
Field visits, 26
Field work, 29, 93–94
Flexibility, 65–66,
  132–33, 151
Focus, 80
Follow up, 84–85, 149
  private, 82–83
Foote Cone & Belding,
  xvi
Franklin, Ben, 100
Freeman, Cliff, 97
Friends, 154

Gardner, Steve, xix, 139
Gardner Nelson &
  Partners, xix, 35, 139
Gettysburg Address, 70,
  122
Gladwell, Malcolm,
  xxv–xxvi, 162
Goal setting, 3–4
Golf, 150
Good work, 38–40
Grace under pressure,
  173, 151
Great work, 38–40
  relationships and,
    97–99

Grief stages, xix
Grooming, 157–60

Handwriting, 128
Handwritten notes, 167
Headlines, 126
Hidden in Plain Sight, 163
Hoffman, Dustin, 91
Hotel
    reservations, 146
    room amenity, 146
HP, 49
Humor, 40, 173

"I have a dream" speech,
    122
Ideas
    ads driven by, 41–42
    generation of, 172,
        174, 175
Ikea, xxvii, 97
Illustrator, 16–17
In-person meetings, 83
Insights, 28
Instinct, 25–26, 171–72
Integrity, 96, 98, 173,
    174, 175
Internal presentations,
    61–62

Joachinshtaler, Erich, 163
Jokes, 125
Jordan, Jay, xvi
Jordan Industries, xvi
Judgment, 55, 89–90,
    173, 174, 175
Juicing the Orange, 163

Kanner, Bernice, 162
Kelley, Tom, 163
Key benefit, 21
Key fact, 21
Killer advertising, 31
King, Martin Luther, 122
Knowledge gaps, 28

Leading, 82–83, 165
Legal agreements, 111–12
Letter of proposal, xxi,
    111–13, 121
        sample, 114–21
Lincoln, Abraham, 122
Listening, 19, 75–76, 98,
    151, 172
Live discussion, 143–44

Mailing quantity, 142
Mandatories, 21, 33, 56
Manhattan Yellow Pages,
    20
Marketing services, xii
McAd, 15
Media, 162
    opportunities, 6–7
    planning, buying,
        117–18
Meeting, 77–78
    agenda, 79–80
    brevity, 81
    defined ending, 83
    leading, 82–83
Messner, Tom, 162, 163
Meticulousness, 174
Mistakes, xxi–xxii
Morale, 104
Motss, Stanley, 91
Myers's rum, 25

Negotiation, 105–6,
    132–33
Nelson, Tom, xix, 35, 36
Network TV, 6
Neumeier, Marty, 163
New business, 170–71
    presentation, 57, 58
New Yorker, The, 125
New York Times, The, 11,
    122
Next steps, 112, 120–21
Nike slogan, xiii
No surprises, xiv

Objective, 21
Ogilvy, David, 9, 161
On-the-job training, 170
On Writing Well, 171
Opening remarks, 69–70
Open-mind, 55–56, 151
Opinions, 73–74, 107
Options, 109
Outdoor billboards, 6
Ownership sense, 98,
    174

Palazzo, Phil, xvi–xvii
Paragraphs, short, 112
Patience, 173
Perfect Pitch, 163
Performance, xxv
Personal agendas, 4
Personal goals, 4
Personal preferences, 56
Photoshop, 123
Pitch team, 63–64
Polaroid, 25
*Polaroid Frequent Smileage
    Program,* 25
Political discussions,
    150–51
Popular culture, 150
PowerPoint, xvi, xxi, 67,
    111, 122–28
Preparation, 67–68,
    71–72, 81
Presentation, 128
    day, 60–62
    flexibility in, 65–66
    opening, 69–70
Presenter, 128
Print, 6
Private follow up, 82–83
Problem, 21
    solving, 98, 108–9
Product
    facts, 33
    launch disclosure,
        139–40

Punctuality, 77–78
Puris, Martin, 27, 28, 89

Qualifying answer, 105–6
Quark, 123
Questioning, 98

Radio, 6
Rapp Collins, xvii–xviii
Rehearsal, 67–68
    presentation, 57–59
Relationship, xxv–xxvi,
    xxviii, 94, 95–96
    breakdowns, 97–99
Religion, 150–51
Representative, xxiii–xxv
Research, 25–26, 73–74
Respect, 53–56
Rewriting, 113
Risk, xxviii
Rules, 89–90
Rush jobs, 11–15

Schedule, 11–15, 112,
    119–20, 132–33
Scheduling delay,
    134–36
Scope creep, 136
Scope of work
    components, 112,
    115–18
Script, throwing away,
    65–66
Seating arrangements,
    147–48
Self-effacement, 174
Self employment, xv–xvi
Self-indulgence, 41–42
Self publishing, xx
Self restraint, 152–53
Selling, 49–50
Senn, Fred, 163
Service, xxv
    economy, xxv
    facts, 33

orientation, 174
Slide customization, 127
Social events, 145–49
Solomon Strategic, xvi
"So what" test, 37, 56
Staples, 97
Statement of desired
    accomplishment, 33
Steel, Jon, 163
Storyboard
    interpretation, 18
Strategy, 32–33, 34,
    11–15, 165
Straw men elimination,
    45
Strunk, William, xxii,
    161, 171
Style assistance, 159
Success, defining, 5
Suede shoes, 159
Support, 21
Szechuan noodles, 35,
    36

Taco Bell, xxvii, 97
Talking, 75–76
Target audience
    language, 40
TBWA/Chiat Day, xxvii,
    97
Teamwork, 100–101
Teleconferences, 83
Television, 6
Template creation,
    123–24
"Thanks for the
    opportunity" closing,
    112, 121
Thank you, 166–68
Thinking, 108, 109
Tipping Point, The, 161,
    182
Tolstoy, Leo, 102
Tone, 21
Trade publications, 30

Transportation
    arrangements, 146–47
Travel wardrobe, 159
Trouble, dealing with,
    xxi–xxii, 137–38
Trust, xxviii, 50
Typographical error,
    13–14

Umbrella theory, 71–72
Uniform, 160
United Airlines, xxvii
Unpleasant surprises, 98
UPS, 31
USA Today, 11

Venture capital partners,
    xvi
Verklin, David, xi–xiv,
    xx–xxi, 162
Vining, W. David, 49
Visual images, 126–27

Wag the Dog, 91
Wall Street, 9
War and Peace, 102
Watch This Listen Up
    Click Here, 162
Web, 6
Web site, 30
White, E.B., xxii, 161, 171
Woods, Tiger, 150
Word documents, 111
Work, xxvi–xxviii
    approval, 54
    bad, 41–42
    good vs. great,
    38–40
    improvement, 54
Working relationship,
    97–99
World Trade Center, xvii
Writer, 27, 28
Writing, 111–13
Zinsser, William, 171

In his 20+ years in the advertising business, Robert Solomon has worked with a wide range of industry leading clients in financial services, technology, and telecommunications, among them American Express, Ameritech, AT&T, Cablevision, Citibank, Columbia Business School, Compaq Computer, DHL, General Motors, Johnson & Johnson, Kaiser Permanente, Levi-Strauss, MasterCard, Mercedes-Benz, Pacific Bell, Polaroid, Seagram, Standard Oil of Ohio, TSYS, UPS, VantageScore, and VISA. For many clients he pioneered brand-enhancing relationship marketing programs.

Robert has conducted workshops and given talks on client service, direct marketing, discipline integration, agency search, and related topics for a wide range of organizations, including the Association of National Advertisers, Columbia University, the Direct Marketing Association, the Direct Marketing Educational Foundation, DM Days, Mercedes-Benz, Messner, and Omnicom.

Robert has a master's degree from the University of North Carolina at Chapel Hill. His undergraduate degree is from George Washington University, where he graduated with honors and as a member of Phi Beta Kappa. He has a certificate in organizational and executive coaching from New York University's school of continuing and professional studies.